The Homeric Hymns

Andrew Lang

Contents

THE HOMERIC HYMNS

BY

Andrew Lang

DEDICATION

To Henry Butcher
A Little Token
of A Long Friendship

PREFACE

To translate the Hymns usually called "Homeric" had long been my wish, and, at the Publisher's suggestion, I undertook the work. Though not in partnership, on this occasion, with my friend, Mr. Henry Butcher (Professor of Greek in the University of Edinburgh), I have been fortunate in receiving his kind assistance in correcting the proofs of the longer and most of the minor Hymns. Mr. Burnet, Professor of Greek in the University of St. Andrews, has also most generously read the proofs of the translation. It is, of course, to be understood that these scholars are not responsible for the slips which may have wandered into my version, the work of one whose Greek has long "rusted in disuse." Indeed I must confess that the rendering "Etin" for [Greek text] is retained in spite of Mr. Butcher, who is also not wholly satisfied with "gledes of light," and with "shieling" for a pastoral summer station in the hills. But I know no word for it in English south of Tweed.

Mr. A. S. Murray, the Head of the Classical Department in the British Museum, has also been good enough to read, and suggest corrections in the preliminary Essays; while Mr. Cecil Smith, of the British Museum, has obligingly aided in selecting the works of art here reproduced.

The text of the Hymns is well known to be corrupt, in places impossible, and much mended by conjecture. I have usually followed Gemoll (Die Homerischen Hymnen, Leipzig, 1886), but have sometimes preferred a MS. reading, or emendations by Mr. Tyrrell, by Mr. Verral, or the admirable suggestions of Mr. Allen. My chief object has been to find, in cases of doubt, the phrases least unworthy of the poets. Too often it is impossible to be certain as to what they really wrote.

I have had beside me the excellent prose translation by Mr. John Edgar (Thin, Edinburgh, 1891). As is inevitable, we do not always agree in the sense of certain phrases, but I am far from claiming superiority for my own attempts.

The method employed in the Essays, the anthropological method of interpreting beliefs and rites, is still, of course, on its trial. What can best be said as to its infirmities, and the dangers of its abuse, and of system-making in the present state of the evidence, will be found in Sir Alfred Lyall's "Asiatic Studies," vol. ii. chaps. iii. and iv. Readers inclined to pursue the subject should read Mr. L. R. Farnell's "Cults of the Greek States" (Clarendon Press, 1896), Mr. J. G. Frazer's "Golden Bough," his "Pausanias," and Mr. Hartland's work on "The Myth of Perseus." These books, it must be observed, are by no means always in agreement with my own provisional theories.

ESSAYS INTRODUCTORY

THE SO-CALLED HOMERIC HYMNS

The existing collection of the Hymns is of unknown editorship, unknown date, and unknown purpose," says Baumeister. Why any man should have collected the little preludes of five or six lines in length, and of purely conventional character, while he did not copy out the longer poems to which they probably served as preludes, is a mystery. The celebrated Wolf, who opened the path which leads modern Homerologists to such an extraordinary number of divergent theories, thought rightly that the great Alexandrian critics before the Christian Era, did not recognise the Hymns as "Homeric." They did not employ the Hymns as illustrations of Homeric problems; though it is certain that they knew the Hymns, for one collection did exist in the third century B.C. {4} Diodorus and Pausanias, later, also cite "the poet in the Hymns," "Homer in the Hymns"; and the pseudo-Herodotus ascribes the Hymns to Homer in his Life of that author. Thucydides, in the Periclean age, regards Homer as the blind Chian minstrel who composed the Hymn to the Delian Apollo: a good proof of the relative antiquity of that piece, but not evidence, of course, that our whole collection was then regarded as Homeric. Baumeister agrees with Wolf that the brief Hymns were recited by rhapsodists as preludes to the recitation of Homeric or other cantos. Thus, in Hymn xxxi. 18, the poet says that he is going on to chant "the renowns of men half divine." Other preludes end with a prayer to the God for luck in the competition of reciters.

This, then, is the plausible explanation of most of the brief Hymns--they were preludes to epic recitations--but the question as to the long narrative Hymns with which the collection opens is different. These were themselves rhapsodies recited at Delphi, at Delos, perhaps in Cyprus (the long Hymn to Aphrodite), in Athens (as the Hymn to Pan, who was friendly in the Persian invasion), and so forth. That the Pisistratidae organised Homeric recitations at Athens is certain enough, and Baumeister suspects, in xiv., xxiii., xxx., xxxi., xxxii., the hand of Onomacritus, the forger of Oracles, that strange accomplice of the Pisistratidae. The Hymn to Aphrodite is just such a lay as the Phaeacian minstrel sang at the feast of Alcinous, in the hearing of Odysseus. Finally Baumeister supposes our collection not to have been made by learned editors, like Aristarchus and Zenodotus, but committed confusedly from memory to papyrus by some amateur. The conventional attribution of the Hymns to Homer, in spite of linguistic objections, and of many allusions to things unknown or unfamiliar in the Epics, is merely the result of the tendency to set down "masterless" compositions to a well-known name. Anything of epic characteristics was allotted to the master of Epic. In the same way an unfathered joke of Lockhart's was attributed to Sydney Smith, and the process is constantly illustrated in daily conversation. The word [Greek text], hymn, had not originally a religious sense: it merely meant a lay. Nobody calls the Theocritean idylls on Heracles and the Dioscuri "hymns," but they are quite as much "hymns" (in our sense) as the "hymn" on Aphrodite, or on Hermes.

To the English reader familiar with the Iliad and Odyssey the Hymns must appear disappointing, if he come to them with an expectation of discovering merits like those of the immortal epics. He will not find that they stand to the Iliad as Milton's "Ode to the Nativity" stands to "Paradise Lost." There is in the Hymns, in fact, no scope for the epic knowledge of human nature in every mood and aspect. We are not so much interested in the Homeric Gods as in the Homeric mortals, yet the Hymns are chiefly concerned not with men, but with Gods and their mythical adventures. However, the interest of the Hymn to Demeter is perfectly human, for the Goddess is in sorrow, and is mingling with men. The Hymn to Aphrodite, too, is Homeric in its grace, and charm, and divine sense of human limitations, of old age that comes on the fairest, as Tithonus and Anchises; of death and disease that wait for all. The life of the Gods is one long holiday; the end of our holiday is always near at hand. The Hymn to Dionysus, representing him as a youth in the fulness of beauty, is of a charm which was not attainable, while early art represented the God as a mature man; but literary art, in the Homeric age, was in advance of sculpture and painting. The chief merit of the Delian Hymn is in the concluding description of the assembled Ionians, happy seafarers like the Phaeacians in the morning of the world. The confusions of the Pythian Hymn to Apollo make it less agreeable; and the humour of the Hymn to Hermes is archaic. All those pieces, however, have delightfully fresh descriptions of sea and land, of shadowy dells, flowering meadows, dusky, fragrant caves; of the mountain glades where the wild beasts fawn in the train of the winsome Goddess; and the high still peaks where Pan wanders among the nymphs, and the glens where Artemis drives the deer, and the spacious halls and airy palaces of the Immortals. The Hymns are fragments of the work of a school which had a great Master and great traditions: they also illustrate many aspects of Greek religion.

In the essays which follow, the religious aspect of the Hymns is chiefly dwelt upon: I endeavour to bring out what Greek religion had of human and sacred, while I try to explain its less majestic features as no less human: as derived from the earliest attempts at speculation and at mastering the secrets of the world. In these chapters regions are visited which scholars have usually neglected or ignored. It may seem strange to seek the origins of Apollo, and of the renowned Eleusinian Mysteries, in the tales and rites of the Bora and the Nanga; in the beliefs and practices of Pawnees and Larrakeah, Yao and Khond. But these tribes, too, are human, and what they now or lately were, the remote ancestors of the Greeks must once have been. All races have sought explanations of their own ritual in the adventures of the Dream Time, the **Alcheringa**, when beings of a more potent race, Gods or Heroes, were on earth, and achieved and endured such things as the rites commemorate. And the things thus endured and achieved, as I try to show, are everywhere of much the same nature; whether they are now commemorated by painted savages in the Bora or the Medicine Dance, or whether they were exhibited and proclaimed by the Eumolpidae in a splendid hall, to the pious of Hellas and of Rome. My attempt may seem audacious, and to many scholars may even be repugnant; but it is on these lines, I venture to think, that the darker problems of Greek religion and rite must be approached. They are all survivals, however fairly draped and adorned by the unique genius of the most divinely gifted race of mankind.

The method of translation is that adopted by Professor Butcher and myself in the Odyssey, and by me in a version of Theocritus, as well as by Mr. Ernest Myers, who preceded us, in his Pindar. That method has lately been censured and, like all methods, is open to objection. But I confess that neither criticism nor example has converted me to the use of modern colloquial English, and I trust that my persistence in using poetical English words in the translation of Greek poetry will not greatly offend. I cannot render a speech of Anchises thus:--

> "If you really are merely a mortal, and if a woman of the normal kind was your mother, while your father (as you lay it down) was the well-known Otreus, and if you come here all through an undying person, Hermes; and if you are to be known henceforward as my wife,--why, then nobody, mortal or immortal, shall interfere with my intention to take instant advantage of the situation."

That kind of speech, though certainly long-winded, may be the manner in which a contemporary pastoralist would address a Goddess "in a coming on humour." But the situation does not occur in the prose of our existence, and I must prefer to translate the poet in a manner more congenial, if less up to date. For one rare word "Etin" ([Greek text]) I must apologise: it seems to me to express the vagueness of the unfamiliar monster, and is old Scots, as in the tale of "The Red Etin of Ireland."

THE HYMN TO APOLLO

The Hymn to Apollo presents innumerable difficulties, both of text, which is very corrupt, and as to the whole nature and aim of the composition. In this version it is divided into two portions, the first dealing with the birth of Apollo, and the foundation of his shrine in the isle of Delos; the second concerned with the establishment of his Oracle and fane at Delphi. The division is made merely to lighten the considerable strain on the attention of the English reader. I have no pretensions to decide whether the second portion was by the author of the first, or is an imitation by another hand, or is contemporary, or a later addition, or a mere compilation from several sources. The first part seems to find a natural conclusion, about lines 176-181. The blind singer (who is quoted here by Thucydides) appears at that point to say farewell to his cherished Ionian audience. What follows, in our second part, appeals to hearers interested in the Apollo of Crisa, and of the Delphian temple: the *Pythian* Apollo.

According to a highly ingenious, but scarcely persuasive theory of Mr. Verrall's, this interest is unfriendly. {13} Our second part is no hymn at all, but a sequel tacked on for political purposes only: and valuable for these purposes because so tacked on.

From line 207 to the end we have this sequel, the story of Apollo's dealings as Delphinian, and as Pythian; all this following on detached fragments of enigmatic character, and containing also (305-355) the intercalated myth about the birth of Typhaon from Hera's anger. In the politically inspired sequel there is, according to Mr. Verrall, no living zeal for the honour of Pytho (Delphi). The threat of the God to his Cretan ministers,--"Beware of arrogance, or . . . "--must be a prophecy after the event. Now such an event occurred, early in the sixth century, when the Crisaeans were supplanted by the people of the town that had grown up round the

Oracle at Delphi. In them, and in the Oracle under their management, the poet shows no interest (Mr. Verrall thinks), none in the many mystic peculiarities of the shrine. It is quite in contradiction with Delphian tradition to represent, as the Hymn does, Trophonius and Agamedes as the *original* builders.

Many other points are noted--such as the derivation of "Pytho" from a word meaning *rot*,--to show that the hymnist was rather disparaging than celebrating the Delphian sanctuary. Taking the Hymn as a whole, more is done for Delos in three lines, says Mr. Verrall, than for Pytho or Delphi in three hundred. As a whole, the spirit of the piece is much more Delian (Ionian) than Delphic. So Mr. Verrall regards the *Cento* as "a religious pasquinade against the sanctuary on Parnassus," a pasquinade emanating from Athens, under the Pisistratidae, who, being Ionian leaders, had a grudge against "the Dorian Delphi," "a comparatively modern, unlucky, and from the first unsatisfactory" institution. Athenians are interested in the "far-seen" altar of the seaman's Dolphin God on the shore, rather than in his inland Pythian habitation.

All this, with much more, is decidedly ingenious. If accepted it might lead the way to a general attack on the epics, as *tendenz* pieces, works with a political purpose, or doctored for a political purpose. But how are we to understand the uses of the pasquinade Hymn? Was it published, so to speak, to amuse and aid the Pisistratidae? Does such remote antiquity show us any examples of such handling of sacred things in poetry? Might we not argue that Apollo's threat to the Crisaeans was meant by the poet as a friendly warning, and is prior to the fall of Crisa? One is reminded of the futile ingenuity with which German critics, following their favourite method, have analysed the fatal Casket Letters of Mary Stuart into letters to her husband, Darnley; or to Murray; or by Darnley to Mary, with scraps of her diary, and false interpolations. The enemies of the Queen, coming into possession of her papers after the affair of Carberry Hill, falsified the Casket Letters into their present appearance of unity. Of course historical facts make this ingenuity unavailing. We regret the circumstance in the interest of the Queen's reputation, but welcome these illustrative examples of what can be done in Germany. {16a}

Fortunately all Teutons are not so ingenious. Baumeister has fallen on those who, in place of two hymns, Delian and Pythian, to Apollo, offer us half-a-dozen fragments. By presenting an array of discordant conjectures as to the number and nature of these scraps, he demonstrates the purely wilful and arbitrary nature of the critical method employed. {16b} Thus one learned person believes in (1) two perfect little poems; (2) two larger hymns; (3) three lacerated fragments of hymns, one lacking its beginning, the other wofully deprived of its end. Another *savant* detects no less than eight fragments, with interpolations; though perhaps no biblical critic *ejusdem farinae* has yet detected eight Isaiahs. There are about ten other theories of similar plausibility and value. Meanwhile Baumeister argues that the Pythian Hymn (our second part) is an imitation of the Delian; by a follower, not of Homer, but of Hesiod. Thus, the Hesiodic school was closely connected with Delphi; the Homeric with Ionia, so that Delphi rarely occurs in the Epics; in fact only thrice (I. 405, [Greek text]. 80, [Greek text]. 581). The local knowledge is accurate (Pythian Hymn, 103 *sqq*.). These are local legends, and knowledge of the curious chariot ritual of Onchestus. The Muses are united with the Graces as in a work of art in the Delphian temple. The poet chooses the Hesiodic and un-Homeric myth of Heaven and Earth, and their progeny: a myth current also in Polynesia, Australia, and New Zealand. The poet is full of inquiry as to origins, even etymological, as is Hesiod. Like Hesiod (and Mr. Max Muller), *origines rerum ex nominibus explicat*. Finally, the second poet (and here every one must agree) is a much worse poet than the first. As for the prophetic word of warning to the Crisaeans and its fulfilment, Baumeister urges that the people of Cirrha, the seaport, not of Crisa, were punished, in Olympiad 47 (Grote, ii. 374).

Turning to Gemoll, we find him maintaining that the two parts were in ancient times regarded as one hymn in the age of Aristophanes. {18} If so, we can only reply, if we agree with Baumeister, that in the age of Aristophanes, or earlier, there was a plentiful lack of critical discrimination. As to Baumeister's theory that the second part is Hesiodic, Gemoll finds a Hesiodic reminiscence in the first part (line 121), while there are Homeric reminiscences in the second part.

Thus do the learned differ among themselves, and an ordinary reader feels tempted to rely on his own literary taste.

According to that criterion, I think we probably have in the Hymn the work of a good poet, in the early part; and in the latter part, or second Hymn, the work of a bad poet, selecting unmanageable passages of myth, and handling them pedantically and ill. At all events we have here work visibly third rate, which cannot be said, in my poor opinion, about the immense mass of the Iliad and Odyssey. The great Alexandrian critics did not use the Hymns as illustrative material in their discussion of Homer. Their instinct was correct, and we must not start the consideration of the Homeric question from these much neglected pieces. We must not study *obscurum per obscurius*. The genius of the Epic soars high above such myths as those about Pytho, Typhaon, and the Apollo who is alternately a dolphin and a meteor: soars high above pedantry and bad etymology. In the Epics we breathe a purer air.

Descending, as it did, from the mythology of savages, the mythic store of Greece was rich in legends such as we find among the lowest races. Homer usually ignores them: Hesiod and the authors of the Hymns are less noble in their selections.

For this reason and for many others, we regard the Hymns, on the whole, as post-Homeric, while their collector, by inserting the Hymn to Ares, shows little proof of discrimination. Only the methods of modern German scholars, such as Wilamowitz Mollendorf, and of Englishmen like Mr. Walter Leaf, can find in the Epics marks of such confusion, dislocation, and interpolations as confront us in the Hymn to Apollo. (I may refer to my work, "Homer and the Epic," for a defence of the unity of Iliad and Odyssey.) For example, Mr. Verrall certainly makes it highly probable that the Pythian Hymn, at least in its concluding words of the God, is not earlier than the sixth century. But no proof of anything like this force is brought against the antiquity of the Iliad or Odyssey.

As to the myths in the Hymns, I would naturally study them from the standpoint of anthropology, and in the light of comparison of the legends of much more backward peoples than the Greeks. But that light at present is for me broken and confused.

I have been led to conclusions varying from those of such students as Mr. Tylor and Mr. Spencer, and these conclusions should be stated, before they are applied to the Myth of Apollo. I am not inclined, like them, to accept "Animism," or "The Ghost Theory," as the master-key to the *origin* of religion, though Animism is a great tributary stream. To myself it now appears that among the lowest known races we find present a fluid mass of beliefs both high and low, from the belief in a moral creative being, a judge of men, to the pettiest fable which envisages him as a medicine-man, or even as a beast or bird. In my opinion the higher belief may very well be the earlier. While I can discern the processes by which the lower myths were evolved, and were attached to a worthier pre-existing creed, I cannot see how, if the lower faiths came first, the higher faith was ever evolved out of *them* by very backward savages.

On the other side, in the case of Australia, Mr. Tylor writes: "For a long time after Captain Cook's visit, the information as to native religious ideas is of the scantiest." This was inevitable, for our information has only been obtained with the utmost difficulty, and under promises of secrecy, by later inquirers who had entirely won the confidence of the natives, and had been initiated into their Mysteries. Mr. Tylor goes on in the same sentence: "But, since the period of European colonists and missionaries, a crowd of alleged native names for the Supreme Deity and a great Evil Deity have been recorded, which, if really of native origin, would show the despised black fellow as in possession of theological generalisations as to the formation and conservation of the universe, and the nature of good and evil, comparable with those of his white supplanter in the land." {23a} Mr. Tylor then proceeds to argue that these ideas have been borrowed from missionaries. I have tried to reply to this argument by proving, for example, that the name of Baiame, one of these deities, could not have been borrowed (as Mr. Tylor seems inclined to hold) from a missionary tract published sixteen years after we first hear of Baiame, who, again, was certainly dominant before the arrival of missionaries. I have adduced other arguments of the same tendency, and I will add that the earliest English explorers and missionaries in Virginia and New England (1586-1622) report from America beliefs absolutely parallel in many ways to the creeds now reported from Australia. Among these notions are "ideas of moral judgment and retribution after death," which in Australia Mr. Tylor marks as "imported." {23b} In my opinion the certainty that the beliefs in America were not imported, is another strong argument for their native character, when they are found with such striking resemblances among the very undeveloped savages of Australia.

Savages, Mr. Hartland says in a censure of my theory, are "guiltless" of Christian teaching. {24} If Mr. Hartland is right, Mr. Tylor is wrong; the ideas, whatever else they are, are unimported, yet, *teste* Mr. Tylor, the ideas are comparable with those of the black man's white supplanters. I would scarcely go so far. If we take, however, the best ideas attributed to the blacks, and hold them disengaged from the accretion of puerile fables with which they are overrun, then there are discovered notions of high religious value, undeniably analogous to some Christian dogmas. But the sanction of the Australian gods is as powerfully lent to silly, or cruel, or needless ritual, as to some moral ideas of weight and merit. In brief, as far as I am able to see, all sorts of ideas, the lowest and the highest, are held at once confusedly by savages, and the same confusion survives in ancient Greek belief. As far back as we can trace him, man had a wealth of religious and mythical conceptions to choose from, and different peoples, as they advanced in civilisation, gave special prominence to different elements in the primal stock of beliefs. The choice of Israel was unique: Greece retained far more of the lower ancient ideas, but gave to them a beauty of grace and form which is found among no other race.

If this view be admitted for the moment, and for the argument's sake, we may ask how it applies to the myths of Apollo. Among the ideas which even now prevail among the backward peoples still in the neolithic stage of culture, we may select a few conceptions. There is the conception of a great primal anthropomorphic Being, who was in the beginning, or, at least, about whose beginning legend is silent. He made all things, he existed on earth (in some cases), teaching men the arts of life and rules of conduct, social and moral. In those instances he retired from earth, and now dwells on high, still concerned with the behaviour of the tribes.

This is a lofty conception, but it is entangled with a different set of legends. This primal Being is mixed up with strange persons of a race earlier than man, half human, half bestial. Many things, in some cases almost all things, are mythically regarded, not as created, but as the results of adventures and metamorphoses among the members of this original race. Now in New Zealand, Polynesia, Greece, and elsewhere, but not, to my knowledge, in the very most backward peoples, the place of this original race, "Old, old Ones," is filled by great natural objects, Earth, Sky, Sea, Forests, regarded as beings of human parts and passions.

The present universe is mythically arranged in regard to their early adventures: the separation of sky and earth, and so forth. Where this belief prevails we find little or no trace of the primal maker and master, though we do find strange early metaphysics of curiously abstract quality (Maoris, Zunis, Polynesians). As far as our knowledge goes, Greek mythology springs partly from this stratum of barbaric as opposed to strictly savage thought. Ouranos and Gaea, Cronos, and the Titans represent the primal beings who have their counterpart in Maori and Wintu legend. But these, in the Greece of the Epics and Hesiod, have long been subordinated to Zeus and the Olympians, who are envisaged as triumphant gods of a younger generation. There is no Creator; but Zeus--how, we do not know--has come to be regarded as a Being relatively Supreme, and as, on occasion, the guardian of morality. Of course his conduct, in myth, is represented as a constant violation of the very rules of life which he expects mankind to observe. I am disposed to look on this essential contradiction as the result of a series of mythical accretions on an original conception of Zeus in his higher capacity. We can see how the accretions arose. Man never lived consistently on the level of his best original ideas: savages also have endless myths of Baiame or Daramulun, or Bunjil, in which these personages, though interested in human behaviour, are puerile, cruel, absurd, lustful, and so on. Man will sport thus with his noblest intuitions.

In the same way, in Christian Europe, we may contrast Dunbar's pious "Ballat of Our Lady" with his "Kynd Kittok," in which God has his eye on the soul of an intemperate ale-wife who has crept into Paradise. "God lukit, and saw her lattin in, and leugh His heart sair." Examples of this kind of sportive irreverence are common enough; their root is in human nature: and they could not be absent in the mythology of savage or of ancient peoples. To Zeus the myths of this kind would come to be attached in several ways.

As a nature-god of the Heaven he marries the Earth. The tendency of men being to claim descent from a God, for each family with this claim a myth of a separate divine amour was needed. Where there had existed Totemism, or belief in kinship with beasts, the myth of the amour of a wolf, bull, serpent, swan, and so forth, was attached to the legend of Zeus. Zeus had been that swan, serpent, wolf, or bull. Once more, ritual arose, in great part, from the rites of sympathetic magic.

This or that mummery was enacted by men for a magical purpose, to secure success in the chase, agriculture, or war. When the performers asked, "Why do we do thus and thus?" the answer was, "Zeus first did so," or Demeter, or Apollo did so, on a certain occasion. About that occasion a myth was framed, and finally there was no profligacy, cruelty, or absurdity of which the God was not guilty. Yet, all the time, he punished adultery, inhospitality, perjury, incest, cannibalism, and other excesses, of which, in legend, he was always setting the example. We know from Xenophanes, Plato, and St. Augustine how men's consciences were tormented by this unceasing contradiction: this overgrowth of myth on the stock of an idea originally noble. It is thus that I would attempt to account for the contradictory conceptions of Zeus, for example.

As to Apollo, I do not think that mythologists determined to find, in Apollo, some deified aspect of Nature, have laid stress enough on his counterparts in savage myth. We constantly find, in America, in the Andaman Isles, and in Australia, that, subordinate to the primal Being, there exists another who enters into much closer relations with mankind. He is often concerned with healing and with prophecy, or with the inspiration of conjurers or shamans. Sometimes he is merely an under-ling, as in the case of the Massachusetts Kiehtan, and his more familiar subordinate, Hobamoc. {30} But frequently this go-between of God and Man is (like Apollo) the *Son* of the primal Being (often an unbegotten Son) or his Messenger (Anda-man, Noongaburrah, Kurnai, Kamilaroi, and other Australian tribes). He reports to the somewhat otiose primal Being about men's conduct, and he sometimes super-intends the Mysteries. I am disposed to regard the prophetic and oracular Apollo (who, as the Hymn to Hermes tells us, alone knows the will of Father Zeus) as the Greek modification of this personage in savage theology. Where this Son is found in Australia, I by no means regard him as a savage refraction from Christian teaching about a mediator, for Christian teaching, in fact, has not been accepted, least of all by the highly conservative sorcerers, or shamans, or wirreenuns of the tribes. Eu-ropean observers, of course, have been struck by (and have probably exaggerated in some instances) the Christian analogy. But if they had been as well acquainted with ancient Greek as with Christian theology they would have remarked that the Anda-man, American, and Australian "mediators" are infinitely more akin to Apollo, in his relations with Zeus and with men, than to any Person about whom missionaries can preach. But the most devoted believer in borrowing will not say that, when the Australian mediator, Tundun, son of Mungun-gnaur, turns into a porpoise, the Kurnai have borrowed from our Hymn of the Dolphin Apollo. It is absurd to main-tain that the Son of the God, the go-between of God and men, in savage theology, is borrowed from missionaries, while this being has so much more in common with Apollo (from whom he cannot conceivably be borrowed) than with Christ. The Tundun-porpoise story seems to have arisen in gratitude to the porpoise, which drives fishes inshore, for the natives to catch. Neither Tharamulun nor Hobamoc

(Australian and American Gods of healing and soothsaying), who appear to men as serpents, are borrowed from Asclepius, or from the Python of Apollo. The processes have been quite different, and in Apollo, the oracular son of Zeus, who declares his counsel to men, I am apt to see a beautiful Greek modification of the type of the mediating Son of the primal Being of savage belief, adorned with many of the attributes of the Sun God, from whom, however, he is fundamentally distinct. Apollo, I think, is an adorned survival of the Son of the God of savage theology. He was not, at first, a Nature God, solar or not. This opinion, if it seems valid, helps to account, in part, for the animal metamorphoses of Apollo, a survival from the mental confusion of savagery. Such a confusion, in Greece, makes it necessary for the wise son of Zeus to seek information, as in the Hymn to Hermes, from an old clown. This medley of ideas, in the mind of a civilised poet, who believes that Apollo is all-knowing in the counsels of eternity, is as truly mythological as Dunbar's God who laughs his heart sore at an ale-house jest. Dunbar, and the author of the Hymn, and the savage with his tale of Tundun or Daramulun, have all quite contradictory sets of ideas alternately present to their minds; the mediaeval poet, of course, being conscious of the contradiction, which makes the essence of his humour, such as it is. To Greece, in its loftier moods, Apollo was, despite his myth, a noble source of inspiration, of art, and of conduct. But the contradiction in the low myth and high doctrine of Apollo, could never be eradicated under any influence less potent than that of Christianity. {34} If this theory of Apollo's origin be correct, many pages of learned works on Mythology need to be rewritten.

THE HYMN TO HERMES

The Hymn to Hermes is remarkable for the corruption of the text, which appears even to present *lacunae*. The English reader will naturally prefer the lively and charming version of Shelley to any other. The poet can tell and adorn the story without visibly floundering in the pitfalls of a dislocated text. If we may judge by line 51, and if Greek musical tradition be correct, the date of the Hymn cannot be earlier than the fortieth Olympiad. About that period Terpander is said to have given the lyre seven strings (as Mercury does in the poem), in place of the previous four strings. The date of Terpander is dubious, but probably the seven-stringed lyre had long been in common use before the poet attributed the invention to Hermes. The same argument applies to the antiquity of writing, assigned by poets as the invention of various mythical and prehistoric heroes. But the poets were not careful archaeologists, and regarded anachronisms as genially as did Shakespeare or Scott. Moreover, the fact that Terpander did invent the seven chords is not beyond dispute historically, while, mythically, Apollo and Amphion are credited with the idea. That Hermes invented fire-sticks seems a fable which robs Prometheus of the honour. We must not look for any kind of consistency in myth.

The learned differ as to the precise purpose of the Hymn, and some even exclude the invention of the *cithara*. To myself it seems that the poet chiefly revels in a very familiar subject of savage humour (notably among the Zulus), the extraordinary feats and tricks of a tiny and apparently feeble and helpless person or animal, such as Brer Rabbit. The triumph of astuteness over strength (a triumph here assigned to the infancy of a God) is the theme. Hermes is here a rustic *doublure* of Apollo, as he was, in fact, mainly a rural deity, though he became the Messenger of the Gods, and the Guide of Souls outworn. In these respects he answers to the Australian Grogoragally, in his double relation to the Father, Boyma, and to men living and dead. {37a} As a go-between of Gods and men, Hermes may be a *doublure* of Apollo, but, as the Hymn shows, he aspired in vain to Apollo's oracular function. In one respect his behaviour has a singular savage parallel. His shoes woven of twigs, so as not to show the direction in which he is proceeding, answer to the equally shapeless feather sandals of the blacks who "go *Kurdaitcha*," that is, as avengers of blood. I have nowhere else found this practice as to the shoes, which, after all, cannot conceal the direction of the spoor from a native tracker. {37b} The trick of driving the cattle backwards answers to the old legend that Bruce reversed the shoes of his horse when he fled from the court of Edward I.

The humour of the Hymn is rather rustic: cattle theft is the chief joke, cattle theft by a baby. The God, divine as he is, feels his mouth water for roast beef, a primitive conception. In fact, throughout this Hymn we are far from the solemn regard paid to Apollo, from the wistful beauty of the Hymn to Demeter, and from the gladness and melancholy of the Hymn to Aphrodite. Sportive myths are treated sportively, as in the story of Ares and Aphrodite in the Odyssey. Myths contained all conceivable elements, among others that of humour, to which the poet here abandons himself. The statues and symbols of Hermes were inviolably sacred; as Guide of Souls he played the part of comforter and friend: he brought men all things lucky and fortunate: he made the cattle bring forth abundantly: he had the golden wand of wealth. But he was also tricksy as a Brownie or as Puck; and that fairy aspect of his character and legend, he being the midnight thief whose maraudings account for the unexplained disappearances of things, is the chief topic of the gay and reckless hymn. Even the Gods, even angry Apollo, are moved to laughter, for over sport and playfulness, too, Greek religion throws her sanction. At the dishonesties of commerce (clearly regarded as a form of theft) Hermes winks his laughing eyes (line 516). This is not an early Socialistic protest against "Commercialism." The early traders, like the Vikings, were alternately pirates and hucksters, as opportunity served. Every occupation must have its heavenly patron, its departmental deity, and Hermes protects thieves and raiders, "minions of the moon," "clerks of St. Nicholas." His very birth is a stolen thing, the darkling fruit of a divine amour in a dusky cavern. *Il chasse de race*. {39}

THE HYMN TO APHRODITE

The Hymn to Aphrodite is, in a literary sense, one of the most beautiful and quite the most Homeric in the collection. By "Homeric" I mean that if we found the adventure of Anchises occurring at length in the Iliad, by way of an episode, perhaps in a speech of AEneas, it would not strike us as inconsistent in tone, though occasionally in phrase. Indeed the germ of the Hymn occurs in Iliad, B. 820: "AEneas, whom holy Aphrodite bore to the embraces of Anchises on the knowes of Ida, a Goddess couching with a mortal." Again, in E. 313, AEneas is spoken of as the son of Aphrodite and the neat-herd, Anchises. The celebrated prophecy of the future rule of the children of AEneas over the Trojans (Y. 307), probably made, like many prophecies, after the event, appears to indicate the claim of a Royal House at Ilios, and is regarded as of later date than the general context of the epic. The AEneid is constructed on this hint; the Romans claiming to be of Trojan descent through AEneas. The date of the composition cannot be fixed from considerations of the Homeric tone; thus lines 238-239 may be a reminiscence of Odyssey, [Greek text]. 394, and other like suggestions are offered. {41} The conjectures as to date vary from the time of Homer to that of the *Cypria*, of Mimnermus (the references to the bitterness of loveless old age are in his vein) of Anacreon, or even of Herodotus and the Tragedians. The words [Greek text], [Greek text], and other indications are relied on for a late date: and there are obvious coincidences with the Hymn to Demeter, as in line 174, *Demeter* 109, f. Gemoll, however, takes this hymn to be the earlier.

About the place of composition, Cyprus or Asia Minor, the learned are no less divided than about the date. Many of the grounds on which their opinions rest appear unstable. The relations of Aphrodite to the wild beasts under her wondrous spell, for instance, need not be borrowed from Circe with her attendant beasts. If not of Homer's age, the Hymn is markedly successful as a continuation of the Homeric tone and manner.

Modern Puritanism naturally "condemns" Aphrodite, as it "condemns" Helen. But Homer is lenient; Helen is under the spell of the Gods, an unwilling and repentant tool of Destiny; and Aphrodite, too, is driven by Zeus into the arms of a mortal. She is [Greek text], shamefast; and her adventure is to her a bitter sorrow (199, 200). The dread of Anchises--a man is not long of life who lies with a Goddess--refers to a belief found from Glenfinlas to Samoa and New Caledonia, that the embraces of the spiritual ladies of the woodlands are fatal to men. The legend has been told to me in the Highlands, and to Mr. Stevenson in Samoa, while my cousin, Mr. J. J. Atkinson, actually knew a Kaneka who died in three days after an amour like that of Anchises. The Breton ballad, *Le Sieur Nan*, turns on the same opinion. The amour of Thomas the Rhymer is a mediaeval analogue of the Idaean legend.

Aphrodite has better claims than most Greek Gods to Oriental elements. Herodotus and Pausanias (i. xiv. 6, iii. 23, I) look on her as a being first worshipped by the Assyrians, then by the Paphians of Cyprus, and Phoenicians at Askelon, who communicated the cult to the Cythereans. Cyprus is one of her most ancient sites, and Ishtar and Ashtoreth are among her Oriental analogues. She springs from the sea--

"The wandering waters knew her, the winds and the viewless ways,   And the roses grew rosier, and bluer the sea-blue streams of the   bays."

But the charm of Aphrodite is Greek. Even without foreign influence, Greek polytheism would have developed a Goddess of Love, as did the polytheism of the North (Frigga) and of the Aztecs. The rites of Adonis, the vernal year, are, even in the name of the hero, Oriental. "The name Adonis is the Phoenician *Adon*, 'Lord.'" {44} "The decay and revival of vegetation" inspires the Adonis rite, which is un-Homeric; and was superfluous, where the descent and return of Persephone typified the same class of ideas. To whatever extent contaminated by Phoenician influence, Aphrodite in Homer is purely Greek, in grace and happy humanity.

The origins of Aphrodite, unlike the origins of Apollo, cannot be found in a state of low savagery. She is a departmental Goddess, and as such, as ruling a province of human passion, she belongs to a late development of religion. To Christianity she was a scandal, one of the scandals which are absent from the most primitive of surviving creeds. Polytheism, as if of set purpose, puts every conceivable aspect of life, good or bad, under divine sanction. This is much less the case in the religion of the very backward races. We do not know historically, what the germs of religion were; if we look at the most archaic examples, for instance in Australia or the Andaman Islands, we find neither sacrifice nor departmental deities.

Religion there is mainly a belief in a primal Being, not necessarily conceived as spiritual, but rather as an undying magnified Man, of indefinitely extensive powers. He dwells above "the vaulted sky beyond which lies the mysterious home of that great and powerful Being, who is Bunjil, Baiame, or Daramulun in different tribal languages, but who in all is known by a name the equivalent of the only one used by the Kurnai, which is Mungan-ngaur, or 'Our Father.'" {45} This Father is conceived of in some places as "a very great old man with a long beard," enthroned on, or growing into, a crystal throne. Often he is served by a son or sons (Apollo, Hermes), frequently regarded as spiritually begotten; elsewhere, looked on as the son of the wife of the deity, and as father of the tribe. {46a} Scandals connected with fatherhood, amorous intrigues so abundant in Greek mythology, are usually not reported among the lowest races. In one known case, the deity, Pundjel or Bunjil, takes the wives of Karween, who is changed into a crane. {46b} This is one of the many savage aetiological myths which account for the peculiarities of animals as a result of metamorphosis, in the manner of Ovid. It has been connected with the legend of Bunjil, who is thus envisaged, not as "Our Father" beyond the vault of heaven, who still inspires poets, {46c} but as a wandering, shape-shifting medicine-man. Zeus, the Heavenly Father, of course appears times without number in the same contradictory aspect.

But such anecdotes are either not common, or are not frequently reported, in the faiths of the most archaic of known races. Much more frequently we find the totemistic conception. All the kindreds with animal names (why adopted we do not know) are apt to explain these designations by descent from the animals selected, or by metamorphosis of the primal beasts into men. This collides with the other notions of descent from, or creation or manufacture out of clay, by the primal Being, "Father Ours." Such contradictions are nothing to the savage theologian, who is no reconciler or apologist. But when reconciliation and apology are later found to be desirable, as in Greece, it is easy to explain that we are descended ***both*** from Our

Father, and from a swan, cow, ant, serpent, dog, wolf, or what you will. That beast was Our Father, say Father Zeus, in animal disguise. Thus Greek legends of bestial amours of a God are probably, in origin, not primitive, but scandals produced in the effort to reconcile contradictory myths. The result is a worse scandal, an accretion of more low myths about a conception of the primal Being which was, relatively, lofty and pure.

Again, as aristocracies arose, the chief families desired to be sons of the Father in a special sense: not as common men are. Her Majesty's lineage may thus be traced to Woden! Now each such descent required a separate divine amour, and a new scandalous story of Zeus or Apollo, though Zeus may originally have been as celibate as the Australian Baiame or Noorele are, in some legends. Once more, syncretism came in as a mythopoeic influence. Say that several Australian nations, becoming more polite, amalgamated into a settled people. Then we should have several Gods, the chief Beings of various tribes, say Noorele, Bunjil, Mungan-ngaur, Baiame, Daramulun, Mangarrah, Mulkari, Pinmeheal. The most imposing God of the dominant tribe might be elevated to the sovereignty of Zeus. But, in the new administration, places must be found for the other old tribal Gods. They are, therefore, set over various departments: Love, War, Agriculture, Medicine, Poetry, Commerce, while one or more of the sons take the places of Apollo and Hermes. There appears to be a very early example of syncretism in Australia. Daramulun (Papang, Our Father) is "Master of All," on the coast, near Shoalhaven River. Baiame is "Master of All," far north, on the Barwan. But the locally intermediate tribe of the Wiraijuri, or Wiradthuri, have adopted Baiame, and reduced Daramulun to an exploded bugbear, a merely nominal superintendent of the Mysteries; and the southern Coast Murring have rejected Baiame altogether, or never knew him, while making Daramulun supreme.

One obvious method of reconciling various tribal Gods in a syncretic Olympus, is the genealogical. All are children of Zeus, for example, or grandchildren, or brothers and sisters. Fancy then provides an amour to account for each relationship. Zeus loved Leto, Leda, Europa, and so forth. Thus a God, originally innocent and even moral, becomes a perfect pattern of vice; and the eternal contradiction vexes the souls of Xenophanes, Plato, and St. Augustine. Sacrifices, even human sacrifices, wholly unknown to the most archaic faiths, were made to ghosts of men: and especially of kings, in the case of human sacrifice. Thence they were transferred to Gods, and behold a new scandal, when men began to reflect under more civilised conditions. Thus all these legends of divine amours and sins, or most of them, including the wanton legend of Aphrodite, and all the human sacrifices which survived to the disgrace of Greek religion, are really degrading accessories to the most archaic beliefs. They are products, not of the most rudimentary savage existence, but of the evolution through the lower and higher barbarism. The worst features of savage ritual are different--taking the lines of sorcery, of cruel initiations, and, perhaps, of revival of the licence of promiscuity, or of Group Marriage. Of these things the traces are not absent from Greek faith, but they are comparatively inconspicuous. Buffoonery, as we have seen, exists in all grades of civilised or savage rites, and was not absent from the popular festivals of the mediaeval Church: religion throwing her mantle over every human field of action, as over Folk Medicine. On these lines I venture to explain what seem to me the strange and repugnant elements of the religion of a people so refined, and so capable of high moral ideas, as the Greeks. Aphrodite is personified desire, but religion did not throw her mantle over desire alone; the cloistered life, the frank charm of maidenhood, were as dear to the Greek genius, and were consecrated by the examples of Athene, Artemis, and Hestia. She presides over the pure element of the fire of the hearth, just as in the household did the daughter of the king or chief. Hers are the first libations at feasts (xxviii. 5), though in Homer they are poured forth to Hermes.

We may explain the Gods of the minor hymns in the same way. Pan, for instance, as the son of Hermes, inherits the wild, frolicsome, rural aspect of his character. The Dioscuri answer to the Vedic Asvins, twin rescuers of men in danger on land or sea: perhaps the Evening and Morning Star. Dionysus is another aspect of the joy of life and of the world and the vintaging. Moon and Sun, Selene and Helios, appear as quite distinct from Artemis and Apollo; Gaea, the Earth, is equally distinct from Demeter. The Hymn to Ares is quite un-Homeric in character, and is oddly conceived in the spirit of the Scottish poltroon, who cries to his friend, "Haud me, haud me, or I'll fecht!" The war-god is implored to moderate the martial eagerness of the poet. The original collector here showed lack of discrimination. At no time, however, was Ares a popular God in Greece; in Homer he is a braggart and coward.

THE HYMN TO DEMETER

The beautiful Hymn to Demeter, an example of Greek religious faith in its most pensive and most romantic aspects, was found in the last century (1780), in Moscow. *Inter pullos et porcos latitabat*: the song of the rural deity had found its way into the haunts of the humble creatures whom she protected. A discovery even more fortunate, in 1857, led Sir Charles Newton to a little *sacellum*, or family chapel, near Cnidos. On a platform of rock, beneath a cliff, and looking to the Mediterranean, were the ruins of the ancient shrine: the votive offerings; the lamps long without oil or flame; the Curses, or Dirae, inscribed on thin sheets of lead, and directed against thieves or rivals. The head of the statue, itself already known, was also discovered. Votive offerings, cheap curses, objects of folk-lore rite and of sympathetic magic,--these are connected with the popular, the peasant aspect of the religion of Demeter. She it is to whom pigs are sacrificed: who makes the fields fertile with scattered fragments of their flesh; and her rustic effigy, at Theocritus's feast of the harvest home, stands smiling, with corn and poppies in her hands.

But the Cnidian shrine had once another treasure, the beautiful melancholy statue of the seated Demeter of the uplifted eyes; the mourning mother: the weary seeker for the lost maiden: her child Persephone. Far from the ruins above the sea, beneath the scorched seaward wall of rock: far from the aromatic fragrance of the rock-nourished flowers, from the bees, and the playful lizards, Demeter now occupies her place in the great halls of the British Museum. Like the Hymn, this melancholy and tender work of art is imperfect, but the sentiment is thereby rather increased than impaired. The ancients buried things broken with the dead, that the shadows of tool, or weapon, or vase might be set free, to serve the shadows of their masters in the land of the souls. Broken as they, too, are, the Hymn and the statue are "free among the dead," and eloquent of the higher religion that, in Greece, attached itself to the lost Maiden and the sorrowing Mother. Demeter, in religion, was more than a fertiliser of the fields: Kore, the Maiden, was more than the buried pig, or the seed sown to await its resurrection; or the harvest idol, fashioned of corn-stalks: more even than a symbol of the winter sleep and vernal awakening of the year and the life of nature. She became the "dread Persephone" of the Odyssey,

"A Queen over death and the dead."

In her winter retreat below the earth she was the bride of the Lord of Many Guests, and the ruler "of the souls of men outworn." In this office Odysseus in Homer knows her, though neither Iliad nor Odyssey recognises *Kore* as the maiden Spring, the daughter and companion of Demeter as Goddess of Grain. Christianity, even, did not quite dethrone Persephone. She lives in two forms: first, as the harvest effigy made of corn-stalks bound together, the last gleanings; secondly, as "the Fairy Queen Proserpina," who carried Thomas the Rhymer from beneath the Eildon Tree to that land which lies beyond the stream of slain men's blood.

"For a' the bluid that's shed on earth
Flows through the streams of that countrie."

Thus tenacious of life has been the myth of Mother and Maiden, a natural flower of the human heart, found, unborrowed, by the Spaniards in the maize-fields of Peru. Clearly the myth is a thing composed of many elements, glad and sad as the waving fields of yellow grain, or as the Chthonian darkness under earth where the seed awaits new life in the new year. The creed is practical as the folk-lore of sympathetic magic, which half expects to bring good harvest luck by various mummeries; and the creed is mystical as the hidden things and words unknown which assured Pindar and Sophocles of secure felicity in this and in the future life.

The creed is beautiful as the exquisite profile of the corn-tressed head of Persephone on Syracusan coins: and it is grotesque as the custom which bade the pilgrims to Eleusis bathe in the sea, each with the pig which he was about to sacrifice. The highest religious hopes, the meanest magical mummeries are blended in this religion. That one element is earlier than the other we cannot say with much certainty. The ritual aspect, as concerned with the happy future of the soul, does not appear in Iliad or Odyssey, where the Mysteries are not named. But the silence of Homer is never a safe argument in favour of his ignorance, any more than the absence of allusion to tobacco in Shakspeare is a proof that tobacco was, in his age, unknown.

We shall find that a barbaric people, the Pawnees, hold a mystery precisely parallel to the Demeter legend: a Mystery necessarily unborrowed from Greece. The Greeks, therefore, may have evolved the legend long before Homer's day, and he may have known the story which he does not find occasion to tell. As to what was said, shown, and done in the Eleusinia, we only gather that there was a kind of Mystery Play on the sacred legend; that there were fastings, vigils, sacrifices, secret objects displayed, sacred words uttered; and that thence such men as Pindar and Sophocles received the impression that for them, in this and the future life, all was well, was well for those of pure hearts and hands. The "purity" may partly have been ritual, but was certainly understood, also, as relating to excellence of life. Than such a faith (for faith it is) religion has nothing better to give. But the extreme diligence of scholars and archaeologists can tell us nothing more definite. The impressions on the souls of the initiated may have been caused merely by that dim or splendid religious light of the vigils, and by association with sacred things usually kept in solemn sanctuaries. Again, mere buffoonery (as is common in savage Mysteries) brought the pilgrims back to common life when they crossed the bridge on their return to Athens; just as the buffooneries of Baubo brought a smile to the sad lips of Demeter. Beyond this all is conjecture, and the secret may have been so well kept just because, in fact, there was no secret to keep. {59}

Till the end of the present century, mythologists did not usually employ the method of comparing Greek rites and legends with, first, the sympathetic magic and the fables of peasant folk-lore; second, with the Mysteries and myths of contemporary savage races, of which European folk-lore is mainly a survival. For a study of Demeter from these sides (a study still too much neglected in Germany) readers may consult Mannhardt's works, Mr. Frazer's "Golden Bough," and the present translator's "Custom and Myth," and "Myth, Ritual, and Religion." Mr. Frazer, especially, has enabled the English reader to understand the savage and rural element of sympathetic magic as a factor in the Demeter myth. Meanwhile Mr. Pater has dealt with the higher sentiment, the more religious aspect, of the myth and the rites. I am not inclined to go all lengths with Mr. Frazer's ingenious and learned system, as will be seen, while regretting that the new edition of his "Golden Bough" is not yet accessible.

If we accept (which I do not entirely) Mr. Frazer's theory of the origin of the Demeter myth, there is no finer example of the Greek power of transforming into beauty the superstitions of Barbarism. The explanation to which I refer is contained in Mr. J. G. Frazer's learned and ingenious work, "The Golden Bough." While mythologists of the schools of Mr. Max Muller and Kuhn have usually resolved most Gods and heroes into Sun, Sky, Dawn, Twilight; or, again, into elemental powers of Thunder, Tempest, Lightning, and Night, Mr. Frazer is apt to see in them the Spirit of Vegetation. Osiris is a Tree Spirit or a Corn Spirit (Mannhardt, the founder of the system, however, took Osiris to be the Sun). Balder is the Spirit of the Oak. The oak, "we may certainly conclude, was one of the chief, if not the very chief divinity of the Aryans before the dispersion." {61} If so, the Aryans before the dispersion were on an infinitely lower religious level than those Australian tribes, whose chief divinity is not a gum-tree, but a being named "Our Father," dwelling beyond the visible heavens. When we remember the vast numbers of gods of sky or heaven among many scattered races, and the obvious connection of Zeus with the sky (sub Jove frigido), and the usually assigned sense of the name of Zeus, it is not easy to suppose that he was originally an oak. But Mr. Frazer considers the etymological connection of Zeus with the Sanscrit word for sky, an insufficient reason for regarding Zeus as, in origin, a sky-god. He prefers, it seems, to believe that, as being the wood out of which fire was kindled by some Aryan-speaking peoples, the oak may have come to be called "The Bright or Shining One" (Zeus, Jove), by the ancient Greeks and Italians. {62} The Greeks, in fact, used the laurel (daphne) for making fire, not, as far as I am aware, the oak. Though the oak was the tree of Zeus, the heavens were certainly his province, and, despite the oak of Dodona, and the oak on the Capitol, he is much more generally connected with the sky than with the tree. In fact this reduction of Zeus, in origin, to an oak, rather suggests that the spirit of system is too powerful with Mr. Frazer.

He makes, perhaps, a more plausible case for his reduction of dread Persephone to a Pig. The process is curious. Early agricultural man believed in a Corn Spirit, a spiritual essence animating the grain (in itself no very unworthy conception). But because, as the field is mown, animals in the corn are driven into the last unshorn nook, and then into the open, the beast which rushed out of the last patch was identified with the Corn Spirit in some animal shape, perhaps that of a pig; many other animals occur. The pig has a great part in the ritual of Demeter. Pigs of pottery were found by Sir Charles Newton on her sacred ground. The initiate in the Mysteries brought pigs to Eleusis, and bathed with them in the sea. The pig was sacrificed to her; in fact (though not in our Hymn) she was closely associated with pigs. "We may now ask . . . may not the pig be nothing but the Goddess herself in animal form?" {64a} She would later become anthropomorphic: a lovely Goddess, whose hair, as in the Hymn, is "yellow as ripe corn." But the prior pig could not be shaken off. At the Attic Thesmophoria the women celebrated the Descent and Ascent of Persephone,--a "double" of Demeter. In this rite pigs and other things were thrown into certain caverns. Later, the cold remains of pig were recovered and placed on the altar. Fragments were scattered for luck on the fields with the seed-corn. A myth explained that a flock of pigs were swallowed by Earth when Persephone was ravished by Hades to the lower world, of which matter the Hymn says nothing. "In short, the pigs were Proserpine." {64b} The eating of pigs at the Thesmophoria was "a partaking of the body of the God," though the partakers, one thinks, must have been totally unconscious of the circumstance. We must presume that (if this theory be correct) a very considerable time was needed for the evolution of a pig into the Demeter of the Hymn, and the change is quite successfully complete; a testimony to the transfiguring power of the Greek genius.

We may be inclined to doubt, however, whether the task before the genius of Greece, the task of making Proserpine out of a porker, was really so colossal. The primitive mind is notoriously capable of entertaining, simultaneously, the most contradictory notions. Thus, in the Australian "Legend of Eerin," the mourners implore Byamee to accept the soul of the faithful Eerin into his Paradise, Bullimah. No doubt Byamee heard, yet Eerin is now a little owl of plaintive voice, which ratters warning cries in time of peril. {65} No incongruity of this kind is felt to be a difficulty by the childlike narrators. Now I conceive that, starting with the relatively high idea of a Spirit of the Grain, early man was quite capable of envisaging it both spiritually and in zoomorphic form (accidentally conditioned here into horse, there into goat, pig, or what not). But these views of his need not exclude his simultaneous belief in the Corn Spirit as a being anthropomorphic, "Mother Earth," or "Mother Grain," as we follow the common etymology; or that of Mann-hardt ([Greek text]) [Greek text]="barley-mother"). If I am right, poetry and the higher religion moved from the first on the line of the anthropomorphic Lady of the Harvest and the Corn, Mother Barley: while the popular folk- lore of the Corn Spirit (which found utterance in the mirth of harvesting, and in the magic ritual for ensuring fertility), followed on the line of the pig. At some seasons, and in some ceremonies, the pig represented the genius of the corn: in general, the Lady of the Corn was--Demeter. We really need not believe that the two forms of the genius of the corn were ever *consciously* identified. Demeter never was a Pig! {66}

"The Peruvians, we are told, believed all useful plants to be animated by a divine being who causes their growth," says Mr. Frazer. {67} The genealogical table, then, in my opinion, is:--

```
Divine Being of the Grain.
             |
    +---------+------------------------+
    |                                  |
(Anthropomorphized).            (Zoomorphised).
Mother of Corn.                  Pig, Horse,
    Demeter.                     and so on.
```

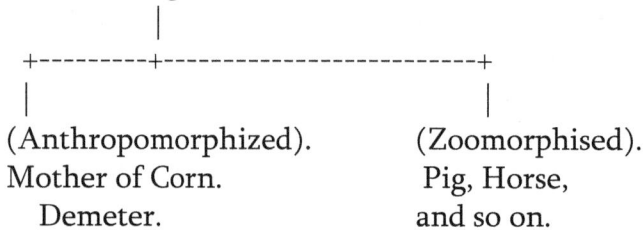

Thus the Greek genius had other and better materials to work on, in evolving Demeter, than the rather lowly animal which is associated with her rites. If any one objects that animal gods always precede anthropomorphic gods in evolution, we reply that, in the most archaic of known races, the deities are represented in human guise at the Mysteries, though there are animal Totems, and though, in myth, the deity may, and often does, assume shapes of bird or beast. {68}

Among rites of the backward races, none, perhaps, so closely resembles the Eleusinian Mysteries as the tradition of the Pawnees. In Attica, Hades, Lord of the Dead, ravishes away Persephone, the vernal daughter of Demeter. Demeter then wanders among men, and is hospitably received by Celeus, King of Eleusis. Baffled in her endeavour to make his son immortal, she demands a temple, where she sits in wrath, blighting the grain. She is reconciled by the restoration of her daughter, at the command of Zeus. But for a third of the year Persephone, having tasted a pomegranate seed in Hades, has to reign as Queen of the Dead, beneath the earth. Scenes from this tale were, no doubt, enacted at the Mysteries, with interludes of buffoonery, such as relieved most ancient and all savage Mysteries. The allegory of the year's death and renewal probably afforded a text for some discourse, or spectacle, concerned with the future life.

Among the Pawnees, not a mother and daughter, but two primal beings, brothers, named Manabozho and Chibiabos, are the chief characters. The Manitos (spirits or gods) drown Chibiabos. Manabozho mourns and smears his face with black, as Demeter wears black raiment. He laments Chibiabos ceaselessly till the Manitos propitiate him with gifts and ceremonies. They offer to him a cup, like the beverage prepared for Demeter, in the Hymn, by Iambe. He drinks it, is glad, washes off the black stain of mourning, and is himself again, while Earth again is joyous. The Manitos restore Chibiabos to life; but, having once died, he may not enter the temple, or "Medicine Lodge." He is sent to reign over the souls of the departed as does Persephone. Manabozho makes offerings to Mesukkumikokwi, the "Earth Mother" of the Pawnees. The story is enacted in the sacred dances of the Pawnees. {69}

The Pawnee ideas have fallen, with singularly accurate coincidence, into the same lines as those of early Greece. Some moderns, such as M. Foucart, have revived the opinion of Herodotus, that the Mysteries were brought from Greece to Egypt. But, as the Pawnee example shows, similar natural phenomena may anywhere beget similar myths and rites. In Greece the *donnee* was a nature myth, and a ritual in which it was enacted. That ritual was a form of sympathetic magic, and the myth explained the performances. The refinement and charm of the legend (on which Homer, as we saw, does not touch) is due to the unique genius of Greece. Demeter became the deity most familiar to the people, nearest to their hearts and endowed with most temples; every farm possessing her rural shrine. But the Chthonian, or funereal, aspect of Chibiabos, or of Persephone, is due to a mood very distinct from that which sacrifices pigs as embodiments of the Corn Spirit, if that be the real origin of the practice.

We should much misconceive the religious spirit of the Greek rite if we undertook to develop it all out an origin in sympathetic magic: which, of course, I do not understand Mr. Frazer to do. Greek scholars, again, are apt to view these researches into savage or barbaric origins with great distaste and disfavour. This is not a scientific frame of mind. In the absence of such researches other purely fanciful origins have been invented by scholars, ancient or modern. It is necessary to return to the pedestrian facts, if merely in order to demonstrate the futility of the fancies. The result is in no way discreditable to Greece. Beginning, like other peoples, with the vague unrealised conception of the Corn Mother (an idea which could not occur before the agricultural stage of civilisation), the Greeks refined and elevated the idea into the Demeter of the Hymn, and of the Cnidian statue. To do this was the result of their unique gifts as a race. Meanwhile the other notion of a Ruler of Souls, in Greece attached to Persephone, is found among peoples not yet agricultural: nomads living on grubs, roots, seeds of wild grasses, and the products of the chase. Almost all men's ideas are as old as mankind, so far as we know mankind.

Conceptions originally "half-conscious," and purely popular, as of a Spirit of Vegetation, incarnate, as it were, in each year's growth, were next handled by conscious poets, like the author of our Hymn, and then are "realised as abstract symbols, because intensely characteristic examples of moral, or spiritual conditions." {72} Thus Demeter and Persephone, no longer pigs or Grain-Mothers, "lend themselves to the elevation and the correction of the sentiments of sorrow and awe, by the presentment to the senses and imagination of an ideal expression of them. Demeter cannot but seem the type of divine grief. Persephone is the Goddess of Death, yet with a promise of life to come."

That the Eleusinia included an ethical element seems undeniable. This one would think probable, *a priori*, on the ground that Greek Mysteries are an embellished survival of the initiatory rites of savages, which do contain elements of morality. This I have argued at some length in "Myth, Ritual, and Religion." Many strange customs in some Greek Mysteries, such as the daubing of the initiate with clay, the use of the [Greek text] (the Australian *Tundun*, a small piece of wood whirled noisily by a string), the general suggestion of *a new life*, the flogging of boys at Sparta, their retreat, each with his instructor (Australian *kabbo*, Greek [Greek text]) to the forests, are precisely analogous to things found in Australia, America, and Africa. Now savage rites are often associated with what we think gross cruelty, and, as in Fiji, with abandoned license, of which the Fathers also accuse the Greeks. But, among the Yao of Central Africa, the initiator, observes Mr. Macdonald, "is said to give much good advice. His lectures condemn selfishness, and a selfish person is called ***mwisichana***, that is, 'uninitiated.'" {74a}

Among the Australians, Dampier, in 1688, observed the singular unselfish generosity of distribution of food to the old, the weak, and the sick. According to Mr. Howitt, the boys of the Coast Murring tribe are taught in the Mysteries "to speak the straightforward truth while being initiated, and are warned to avoid various offences against propriety and morality." The method of instruction is bad, a pantomimic representation of the sin to be avoided, but the intention is excellent. {74b} Among the Kurnai respect for the old, for unprotected women, the duty of unselfishness, and other ethical ideas are inculcated, {74c} while certain food taboos prevail during the rite, as was also the case in the Eleusinia. That this moral idea of "sharing what they have with their friends" is not confined merely to the tribe, is proved by the experience of John Finnegan, a white man lost near Moreton Bay early in this century. "At all times, whether they had much or little, fish or kangaroo, they always gave me as much as I could eat." Even when the whites stole the fish of the natives, and were detected, "instead of attempting to repossess themselves of the fish, they instantly set at work to procure more for us, and one or two fetched us as much ***dingowa*** as they could carry." {75} The first English settlers in Virginia, on the other hand, when some native stole a cup, burned down the whole town.

Thus the morality of the savage is not merely tribal (as is often alleged), and is carried into practice, as well as inculcated, in some regions, not in all, during the Mysteries.

For these reasons, if the Greek Mysteries be survivals of savage ceremonies (as there is no reason to doubt that they are), the savage association of moral instruction with mummeries might survive as easily as anything else. That it did survive is plain from numerous passages in classical authors. {76a} The initiate "live a pious life in regard to strangers and citizens." They are to be "conscious of no evil": they are to "protect such as have wrought no unrighteousness." Such precepts "have their root in the ethico-religious consciousness." {76b} It is not mere ritual purity that the Mysteries demand, either among naked Australians, or Yao, or in Greece. Lobeck did his best to minimise the testimony to the higher element in the Eleusinia, but without avail. The study of early, barbaric, savage, classical, Egyptian, or Indian religions should not be one-sided. Men have always been men, for good as well as for evil; and religion, almost everywhere, is allied with ethics no less than it is overrun by the parasite of myth, and the survival of magic in ritual. The Mother and the Maid were "Saviours" ([Greek text]), "holy" and "pure," despite contradictory legends. {77} The tales of incest, as between Zeus and Persephone, are the result of the genealogical mania. The Gods were grouped in family-relationships, to account for their companionship in ritual, and each birth postulated an amour. None the less the same deities offered "salvation," of a sort, and were patrons of conduct.

Greek religion was thus not destitute of certain chief elements in our own. But these were held in solution, with a host of other warring elements, lustful, cruel, or buffooning. These elements Greece was powerless to shake off; philosophers, by various expedients, might explain away the contradictory myths which overgrew the religion, but ritual, the luck of the State, and popular credulity, were tenacious of the whole strange mingling of beliefs and practices.

* * * *

The view taken of the Eleusinia in this note is hardly so exalted as that of Dr. Hatch. "The main underlying conception of initiation was that there were elements in human life from which the candidate must purify himself before he could be fit to approach God." The need of purification, ritual and moral, is certain, but one is not aware of anything in the purely popular or priestly religion of Greece which exactly answers to our word "God" as used in the passage cited. Individuals, by dint of piety or of speculation, might approach the conception, and probably many did, both in and out of the philosophic schools. But traditional ritual and myth could scarcely rise to this ideal; and it seems exaggerated to say of the crowded Eleusinian throng of pilgrims that "the race of mankind was lifted on to a higher plane when it came to be taught that only the pure in heart can see God." {78} The black native boys in Australia pass through a purgative ceremony to cure them of selfishness, and afterwards the initiator points to the blue vault of sky, bidding them behold "Our Father, Mungan-ngaur." This is very well meant, and very creditable to untutored savages: and creditable ideas were not absent from the Eleusinia. But when we use the quotation, "Blessed are the pure in heart, for they shall see God," our meaning, though not very definite, is a meaning which it would be hazardous to attribute to a black boy,--or to Sophocles. The idea of the New Life appears to occur in Australian Mysteries: a tribesman is buried, and rises at a given signal. But here the New Life is rather that of the lad admitted to full tribal privileges (including moral precepts) than that of a converted character. Confirmation, rather than conversion, is the analogy. The number of those analogies of ancient and savage with Christian religion is remarkable. But even in Greek Mysteries the conceptions are necessarily not so purely spiritual as in the Christian creed, of which they seem half-conscious and fragmentary anticipations. Or we may regard them as suggestions, which Christianity selected, accepted, and purified.

HYMN TO DEMETER
THE ALLEGED EGYPTIAN ORIGINS

In what has been said as to the Greek Mysteries, I have regarded them as of native origin. I have exhibited rites of analogous kinds in the germ, as it were, among savage and barbaric communities. In Peru, under the Incas, we actually find Mama and Cora (Demeter and Kore) as Goddesses of the maize (Acosta), and for rites of sympathetic magic connected with the production of fertile harvests (as in the Thesmophoria at Athens) it is enough to refer to the vast collection in Mr. Frazer's "Golden Bough." I have also indicated the closest of all known parallels to the Eleusinian in a medicine-dance and legend of the Pawnees. For other savage Mysteries in which a moral element occurs, I have quoted Australian and African examples. Thence I have inferred that the early Greeks might, and probably did, evolve their multiform mystic rites out of germs of such things inherited from their own prehistoric ancestors. No process, on the other hand, of borrowing from Greece can conceivably account for the Pawnee and Peruvian rites, so closely analogous to those of Hellas. Therefore I see no reason why, if Egypt, for instance, presents parallels to the Eleusinia, we should suppose that the prehistoric Greeks borrowed the Eleusinia from Egypt. These things can grow up, autochthonous and underived, out of the soil of human nature anywhere, granting certain social conditions. Monsieur Foucart, however, has lately argued in favour of an Egyptian origin of the Eleusinia. {82}

The Greeks naturally identified Demeter and Dionysus with Isis and Osiris. There were analogies in the figures and the legends, and that was enough. So, had the Greeks visited America, they would have recognised Demeter in the Pawnee Earth Mother, and Persephone or Eubouleus in Chibiabos. To account for the similarities they would probably have invented a fable of Pawnee visitors to Greece, or of Greek missionaries among the Pawnees. So they were apt to form a theory of an Egyptian origin of Dionysus and Demeter.

M. Foucart, however, argues that agriculture, corn-growing at least, came into Greece at one stride, barley and wheat not being indigenous in a wild state. The Greeks, however, may have brought grain in their original national migration (the Greek words for grain and ploughing are common to other families of Aryan speech) or obtained it from Phoenician settlements. Demeter, however, in M. Foucart's theory, would be the Goddess of the foreigners who carried the grain first to Hellas. Now both the Homeric epics and the Egyptian monuments show us Egypt and Greece in contact in the Greek prehistoric period. But it does not exactly follow that the prehistoric Greeks would adopt Egyptian gods; or that the Thesmophoria, an Athenian harvest-rite of Demeter, was founded by colonists from Egypt, answering to the daughters of Danaus. {84} Egyptians certainly did not introduce the similar rite among the Khonds, or the Incas. The rites *could* grow up without importation, as the result of the similarities of primitive fancy everywhere. If Isis is Lady of the Grain in Egypt, so is Mama in Peru, and Demeter need no more have been imported from Egypt than Mama. If Osiris taught the arts of life and the laws of society in Egypt, so did Daramulun in Australia, and Yehl in British Columbia. All the gods and culture heroes everywhere play this *role*--in regions where importation of the idea from Egypt is utterly out of the question. Even in minute details, legends recur everywhere; the *phallus* of a mutilated Australian being of the fabulous "Alcheringa time," is hunted for by his wives; exactly as Isis wanders in search of the *phallus* of the mutilated Osiris. {85a} Is anything in the Demeter legend so like the Isis legend as this Australian coincidence? Yet the Arunta did not borrow it from Egypt. {85b} The mere fact, again, that there were Mysteries both in Egypt and Greece proves nothing. There is a river in Monmouth, and a river in Macedon; there are Mysteries in almost all religions.

Again, it is argued, the Gods of the Mysteries in Egypt and Greece had secret names, only revealed to the initiated. So, too, in Australia, women (never initiated) and boys before initiation, know Daramulun only as Papang (Father). {85c} The uninitiated among the Kurnai do not know the sacred name, Mungan-ngaur. {85d} The Australian did not borrow this secrecy from Egypt. Everywhere a mystery is kept up about proper names. M. Foucart seems to think that what is practically universal, a taboo on names, can only have reached Greece by transplantation from Egypt. {86a} To the anthropologist it seems that scholars, in ignoring the universal ideas of the lower races, run the risk of venturing on theories at once superficial and untenable.

M. Foucart has another argument, which does not seem more convincing, though it probably lights up the humorous or indecent side of the Eleusinia. Isocrates speaks of "good offices" rendered to Demeter by "our ancestors," which "can only be told to the initiate." {86b} Now these cannot be the kindly deeds reported in the Hymn, for these were publicly proclaimed. What, then, were the **secret** good offices? In one version of the legend the hosts of Demeter were not Celeus and Metaneira, but Dusaules and Baubo. The part of Baubo was to relieve the gloom of the Goddess, not by the harmless pleasantries of Iambe, in the Hymn, but by obscene gestures. The Christian Fathers, Clemens of Alexandria at least, make this a part of their attack on the Mysteries; but it may be said that they were prejudiced or misinformed. {87a} But, says M. Foucart, an inscription has been found in Paros, wherein there is a dedication to Hera, Demeter Thesmophoros, Kore, and **Babo**, or Baubo. Again, two authors of the fourth century, Palaephatus and Asclepiades, cite the Dusaules and Baubo legend. {87b}

Now the indecent gesture of Baubo was part of the comic or obscene folk- lore of contempt in Egypt, and so M. Foucart thinks that it was borrowed from Egypt with the Demeter legend. {87c} Can Isocrates have referred to **this** good office?-- the amusing of Demeter by an obscene gesture? If he did, such gestures as Baubo's are as widely diffused as any other piece of folk-lore. In the centre of the Australian desert Mr. Carnegie saw a native make a derisive gesture which he thought had only been known to English schoolboys. {88a} Again, indecent pantomimic dances, said to be intended to act as "object lessons" in things **not** to be done, are common in Australian Mysteries. Further, we do not know Baubo, or a counterpart of her, in the ritual of Isis, and the clay figurines of such a figure, in Egypt, are of the Greek, the Ptolemaic period. Thus the evidence comes to this: an indecent gesture of contempt, known in Egypt, is, at Eleusis, attributed to Baubo. This does not prove that Baubo was originally Egyptian. {88b} Certain traditions make Demeter the mistress of Celeus. {88c} Traces of a "mystic marriage," which also occur, are not necessarily Egyptian: the idea and rite are common.

There remains the question of the sacred objects displayed (possibly statues, probably very ancient "medicine" things, as among the Pawnees) and sacred words spoken. These are said by many authors to confirm the initiate in their security of hope as to a future life. Now similar instruction, as to the details of the soul's voyage, the dangers to avoid, the precautions to be taken, notoriously occur in the Egyptian "Book of the Dead." But very similar fancies are reported from the Ojibbeways (Kohl), the Polynesians and Maoris (Taylor, Turner, Gill, Thomson), the early peoples of Virginia, {89a} the modern Arapaho and Sioux of the Ghost Dance rite, the Aztecs, and so forth. In all countries these details are said to have been revealed by men or women who died, but did not (like Persephone) taste the food of the dead; and so were enabled to return to earth. The initiate, at Eleusis, were guided along a theatrically arranged pathway of the dead, into a theatrical Elysium. {89b} Now as such ideas as these occur among races utterly removed from contact with Egypt, as they are part of the European folk-lore of the visits of mortals to fairyland (in which it is fatal to taste fairy food), I do not see that Eleusis need have borrowed such common elements of early belief from the Egyptians in the seventh century B.C. {90} One might as well attribute to Egypt the Finnish legend of the descent of Wainamoinen into Tuonela; or the experience of the aunt of Montezuma just before the arrival of Cortes; or the expedition to fairyland of Thomas the Rhymer. It is not pretended by M. Foucart that the ***details*** of the "Book of the Dead" were copied in Greek ritual; and the general idea of a river to cross, of dangerous monsters to avoid, of perils to encounter, of precautions to be taken by the wandering soul, is nearly universal, where it must be unborrowed from Egypt, in Polynesian and Red Indian belief. As at Eleusis, in these remote tribes formulas of a preservative character are inculcated.

The "Book of the Dead" was a guidebook of the itinerary of Egyptian souls. Very probably similar instruction was given to the initiate at Eleusis. But the Fijians also have a regular theory of what is to be done and avoided on "The Path of the Shades." The shade is ferried by Ceba (Charon) over Wainiyalo (Lethe); he reaches the mystic pandanus tree (here occurs a rite); he meets, and dodges, Drodroyalo and the two devouring Goddesses; he comes to a spring, and drinks, and forgets sorrow at Wai-na-dula, the "Water of Solace." After half-a-dozen other probations and terrors, he reaches the Gods, "the dancing-ground and the white quicksand; and then the young Gods dance before them and sing. . . . " {91a}

Now turn to Plutarch. {91b} Plutarch compares the soul's mortal experience with that of the initiate in the Mysteries. "There are wanderings, darkness, fear, trembling, shuddering, horror, then a marvellous light: pure places and meadows, dances, songs, and holy apparitions." Plutarch might be summarising the Fijian belief. Again, take the mystic golden scroll, found in a Greek grave at Petilia. It describes in hexameters the Path of the Shade: the spring and the white cypress on the left: "Do not approach it. Go to the other stream from the Lake of Memory; tell the Guardians that you are the child of Earth and of the starry sky, but that yours is a heavenly lineage; and they will give you to drink of that water, and you shall reign with the other heroes."

Tree, and spring, and peaceful place with dance, song, and divine apparitions, all are Fijian, all are Greek, yet nothing is borrowed by Fiji from Greece. Many other Greek inscriptions cited by M. Foucart attest similar beliefs. Very probably such precepts as those of the Petilia scroll were among the secret instructions of Eleusis. But they are not so much Egyptian as human. Chibiabos is assuredly not borrowed from Osiris, nor the Fijian faith from the "Book of the Dead." "Sacred things," not to be shown to man, still less to woman, date from the "medicine bag" of the Red Indian, the mystic tribal bundles of the Pawnees, and the *churinga*, and bark "native portmanteaux," of which Mr. Carnegie brought several from the Australian desert.

For all Greek Mysteries a satisfactory savage analogy can be found. These spring straight from human nature: from the desire to place customs, and duties, and taboos under divine protection; from the need of strengthening them, and the influence of the elders, by mystic sanctions; from the need of fortifying and trying the young by probations of strength, secrecy, and fortitude; from the magical expulsion of hostile influences; from the sympathetic magic of early agriculture; from study of the processes of nature regarded as personal; and from guesses, surmises, visions, and dreams as to the fortunes of the wandering soul on its way to its final home. I have shown all these things to be human, universal, not sprung from one race in one region. Greek Mysteries are based on all these natural early conceptions of life and death. The early Greeks, like other races, entertained these primitive, or very archaic ideas. Greece had no need to borrow from Egypt; and, though Egypt was within reach, Greece probably developed freely her original stock of ideas in her own fashion, just as did the Incas, Aztecs, Australians, Ojibbeways, and the other remote peoples whom I have selected. The argument of M. Foucart, I think, is only good as long as we are ignorant of the universally diffused forms of religious belief which correspond to the creeds of Eleusis or of Egypt. In the Greek Mysteries we have the Greek guise,--solemn, wistful, hopeful, holy, and pure, yet not uncontaminated with archaic buffoonery,--of notions and rites, hopes and fears, common to all mankind. There is no other secret.

The same arguments as I have advanced against Greek borrowing from Egypt, apply to Greek borrowing from Asia. Mr. Ramsay, following Mr. Robertson Smith, suggests that Leto, the mother of Apollo and Artemis, may be "the old Semitic Allat." {95a} Then we have Leto and Artemis, as the Mother and the Maid (Kore) with their mystery play. "Clement describes them" (the details) as "Eleusinian, for they had spread to Eleusis as the rites of Demeter and Kore *crossing from Asia to Crete, and from Crete to the European* peninsula." The ritual "remained everywhere fundamentally the same." Obviously if the Eleusinian Mysteries are of Phrygian origin (Ramsay), they cannot also be of Egyptian origin (Foucart). In truth they are no more specially of Phrygian or Egyptian than of Pawnee or Peruvian origin. Mankind can and does evolve such ideas and rites in any region of the world. {95b}

CONCLUSION

What has all this farrago about savages to do with Dionysus?" I conceive some scholar, or literary critic asking, if such an one looks into this book. Certainly it would have been easier for me to abound in aesthetic criticism of the Hymns, and on the aspect of Greek literary art which they illustrate. But the Hymns, if read even through the pale medium of a translation, speak for themselves. Their beauties and defects as poetry are patent: patent, too, are the charm and geniality of the national character which they express. The glad Ionian gatherings; the archaic humour; the delight in life, and love, and nature; the pious domesticities of the sacred Hearth; the peopling of woods, hills, and streams with exquisite fairy forms; all these make the poetic delight of the Hymns. But all these need no pointing out to any reader. The poets can speak for themselves.

On the other hand the confusions of sacred and profane; the origins of the Mysteries; the beginnings of the Gods in a mental condition long left behind by Greece when the Hymns were composed; all these matters need elucidation. I have tried to elucidate them as results of evolution from the remote prehistoric past of Greece, which, as it seems, must in many points have been identical with the historic present of the lowest contemporary races. In the same way, if dealing with ornament, I would derive the spirals, volutes, and concentric circles of Mycenaean gold work, from the identical motives, on the oldest incised rocks and kists of our Islands, of North and South America, and of the tribes of Central Australia, recently described by Messrs. Spencer and Gillen, and Mr. Carnegie. The material of the Mycenaean artist may be gold, his work may be elegant and firm, but he traces the selfsame ornament as the naked Arunta, with feebler hand, paints on sacred rocks or on the bodies of his tribesmen. What is true of ornament is true of myth, rite, and belief. Greece only offers a gracious modification of the beliefs, rites, and myths of the races who now are "nearest the beginning," however remote from that unknown beginning they may be. To understand this is to come closer to a true conception of the evolution of Greek faith and art than we can reach by any other path. Yet to insist on this is not to ignore the unmeasured advance of the Greeks in development of society and art. On that head the Hymns, like all Greek poetry, bear their own free testimony. But, none the less, Greek religion and myth present features repellent to us, which derive their origin, not from savagery, but from the more crude horrors of the lower and higher barbarisms.

Greek religion, Greek myth, are vast conglomerates. We find a savage origin for Apollo, and savage origins for many of the Mysteries. But the cruelty of savage initiations has been purified away. On the other hand, we find a barbaric origin for departmental gods, such as Aphrodite, and for Greek human sacrifices, unknown to the lowest savagery. From savagery Zeus is probably derived; from savagery come the germs of the legends of divine amours in animal forms. But from barbarism arises the sympathetic magic of agriculture, which the lowest races do not practise. From the barbaric condition, not from savagery, comes Greek hero-worship, for the lowest races do not worship ancestral spirits. Such is the medley of prehistoric ideas in Greece, while the charm and poetry of the Hymns are due mainly to the unique genius of the fully developed Hellenic race. The combination of good and bad, of ancestral rites and ideas, of native taste, of philosophical refinement on inherited theology, could not last; the elements were too discordant. And yet it could not pass naturally away. The Greece of A.D. 300

"Wandered between two worlds, one dead,
The other powerless to be born,"

without external assistance. That help was brought by the Christian creed, and, officially, Gods, rites, and myths vanished, while, unofficially, they partially endure, even to this day, in Romaic folk- lore.

HOMERIC HYMNS
HYMN TO APOLLO

Mindful, ever mindful, will I be of Apollo the Far-darter. Before him, as he fares through the hall of Zeus, the Gods tremble, yea, rise up all from their thrones as he draws near with his shining bended bow. But Leto alone abides by Zeus, the Lord of Lightning, till Apollo hath slackened his bow and closed his quiver. Then, taking with her hands from his mighty shoulders the bow and quiver, she hangs them against the pillar beside his father's seat from a pin of gold, and leads him to his place and seats him there, while the father welcomes his dear son, giving him nectar in a golden cup; then do the other Gods welcome him; then they make him sit, and Lady Leto rejoices, in that she bore the Lord of the Bow, her mighty son.

[Hail! O blessed Leto; mother of glorious children, Prince Apollo and Artemis the Archer; her in Ortygia, him in rocky Delos didst thou bear, couching against the long sweep of the Cynthian Hill, beside a palm tree, by the streams of Inopus.]

How shall I hymn thee aright, howbeit thou art, in sooth, not hard to hymn? {104} for to thee, Phoebus, everywhere have fallen all the ranges of song, both on the mainland, nurse of young kine, and among the isles; to thee all the cliffs are dear, and the steep mountain crests and rivers running onward to the salt sea, and beaches sloping to the foam, and havens of the deep? Shall I tell how Leto bore thee first, a delight of men, couched by the Cynthian Hill in the rocky island, in sea-girt Delos--on either hand the black wave drives landward at the word of the shrill winds--whence arising thou art Lord over all mortals?

Among them that dwell in Crete, and the people of Athens, and isle AEgina, and Euboea famed for fleets, and AEgae and Peiresiae, and Peparethus by the sea-strand, and Thracian Athos, and the tall crests of Pelion, and Thracian Samos, and the shadowy mountains of Ida, Scyros, and Phocaea, and the mountain wall of Aigocane, and stablished Imbros, and inhospitable Lemnos, and goodly Lesbos, the seat of Makar son of AEolus, and Chios, brightest of all islands of the deep, and craggy Mimas, and the steep crests of Mykale, and gleaming Claros, and the high hills of AEsagee, and watery Samos, and tall ridges of Mycale, and Miletus, and Cos, a city of Meropian men, and steep Cnidos, and windy Carpathus, Naxos and Paros, and rocky Rheneia--so far in travail with the Archer God went Leto, seeking if perchance any land would build a house for her son.

But the lands trembled sore, and were adread, and none, nay not the richest, dared to welcome Phoebus, not till Lady Leto set foot on Delos, and speaking winged words besought her:

"Delos, would that thou wert minded to be the seat of my Son, Phoebus Apollo, and to let build him therein a rich temple! No other God will touch thee, nor none will honour thee, for methinks thou art not to be well seen in cattle or in sheep, in fruit or grain, nor wilt thou grow plants unnumbered. But wert thou to possess a temple of Apollo the Far- darter; then would all men bring thee hecatombs, gathering to thee, and ever wilt thou have savour of sacrifice . . . from others' hands, albeit thy soil is poor."

Thus spoke she, and Delos was glad and answered her saying:

"Leto, daughter most renowned of mighty Coeus, right gladly would I welcome the birth of the Archer Prince, for verily of me there goes an evil report among men, and thus would I wax mightiest of renown. But at this Word, Leto, I tremble, nor will I hide it from thee, for the saying is that Apollo will be mighty of mood, and mightily will lord it over mortals and immortals far and wide over the earth, the grain-giver. Therefore, I deeply dread in heart and soul lest, when first he looks upon the sunlight, he disdain my island, for rocky of soil am I, and spurn me with his feet and drive me down in the gulfs of the salt sea. Then should a great sea-wave wash mightily above my head for ever, but he will fare to another land, which so pleases him, to fashion him a temple and groves of trees. But in me would many-footed sea-beasts and black seals make their chambers securely, no men dwelling by me. Nay, still, if thou hast the heart, Goddess, to swear a great oath that here first he will build a beautiful temple, to be the shrine oracular of men--thereafter among all men let him raise him shrines, since his renown shall be the widest."

So spake she, but Leto swore the great oath of the Gods:

"Bear witness, Earth, and the wide heaven above, and dropping water of Styx--the greatest oath and the most dread among the blessed Gods--that verily here shall ever be the fragrant altar and the portion of Apollo, and thee will he honour above all."

When she had sworn and done that oath, then Delos was glad in the birth of the Archer Prince. But Leto, for nine days and nine nights continually was pierced with pangs of child-birth beyond all hope. With her were all the Goddesses, the goodliest, Dione and Rheia, and Ichnaean Themis, and Amphitrite of the moaning sea, and the other deathless ones--save white-armed Hera. Alone she wotted not of it, Eilithyia, the helper in difficult travail. For she sat on the crest of Olympus beneath the golden clouds, by the wile of white-armed Hera, who held her afar in jealous grudge, because even then fair-tressed Leto was about bearing her strong and noble son.

But the Goddesses sent forth Iris from the fair-stablished isle, to bring Eilithyia, promising her a great necklet, golden with amber studs, nine cubits long. Iris they bade to call Eilithyia apart from white-armed Hera, lest even then the words of Hera might turn her from her going. But wind-footed swift Iris heard, and fleeted forth, and swiftly she devoured the space between. So soon as she came to steep Olympus, the dwelling of the Gods, she called forth Eilithyia from hall to door, and spake winged words, even all that the Goddesses of Olympian mansions had bidden her. Thereby she won the heart in Eilithyia's breast, and forth they fared, like timid wild doves in their going.

Even when Eilithyia, the helper in sore travailing, set foot in Delos, then labour took hold on Leto, and a passion to bring to the birth. Around a palm tree she cast her arms, and set her knees on the soft meadow, while earth beneath smiled, and forth leaped the babe to light, and all the Goddesses raised a cry. Then, great Phoebus, the Goddesses washed thee in fair water, holy and purely, and wound thee in white swaddling bands, delicate, new woven, with a golden girdle round thee. Nor did his mother suckle Apollo the golden-sworded, but Themis with immortal hands first touched his lips with nectar and sweet ambrosia, while Leto rejoiced, in that she had borne her strong son, the bearer of the bow.

Then Phoebus, as soon as thou hadst tasted the food of Paradise, the golden bands were not proof against thy pantings, nor bonds could bind thee, but all their ends were loosened. Straightway among the Goddesses spoke Phoebus Apollo: "Mine be the dear lyre and bended bow, and I will utter to men the unerring counsel of Zeus."

So speaking, he began to fare over the wide ways of earth, Phoebus of the locks unshorn, Phoebus the Far-darter. Thereon all the Goddesses were in amaze, and all Delos blossomed with gold, as when a hilltop is heavy with woodland flowers, beholding the child of Zeus and Leto, and glad because the God had chosen her wherein to set his home, beyond mainland and isles, and loved her most at heart.

But thyself, O Prince of the Silver Bow, far-darting Apollo, didst now pass over rocky Cynthus, now wander among temples and men. Many are thy fanes and groves, and dear are all the headlands, and high peaks of lofty hills, and rivers flowing onward to the sea; but with Delos, Phoebus, art thou most delighted at heart, where the long-robed Ionians gather in thine honour, with children and shame-fast wives. Mindful of thee they delight thee with boxing, and dances, and minstrelsy in their games. Who so then encountered them at the gathering of the Ionians, would say that they are exempt from eld and death, beholding them so gracious, and would be glad at heart, looking on the men and fair-girdled women, and their much wealth, and their swift galleys. Moreover, there is this great marvel of renown imperishable, the Delian damsels, hand-maidens of the Far-darter. They, when first they have hymned Apollo, and next Leto and Artemis the Archer, then sing in memory of the men and women of old time, enchanting the tribes of mortals. And they are skilled to mimic the notes and dance music of all men, so that each would say himself were singing, so well woven is their fair chant.

But now come, be gracious, Apollo, be gracious, Artemis; and ye maidens all, farewell, but remember me even in time to come, when any of earthly men, yea, any stranger that much hath seen and much endured, comes hither and asks:

"Maidens, who is the sweetest to you of singers here conversant, and in whose song are ye most glad?"

Then do you all with one voice make answer:

"A blind man is he, and he dwells in rocky Chios; his songs will ever have the mastery, ay, in all time to come."

But I shall bear my renown of you as far as I wander over earth to the fairest cities of men, and they will believe my report, for my word is true. But, for me, never shall I cease singing of Apollo of the Silver Bow, the Far-darter, whom fair-tressed Leto bore.

O Prince, Lycia is thine, and pleasant Maeonia, and Miletus, a winsome city by the sea, and thou, too, art the mighty lord of sea-washed Delos.

THE FOUNDING OF DELPHI

The son of glorious Leto fares harping on his hollow harp to rocky Pytho, clad in his fragrant raiment that waxes not old, and beneath the golden plectrum winsomely sounds his lyre. Thence from earth to Olympus, fleet as thought, he goes to the House of Zeus, into the Consistory of the other Gods, and anon the Immortals bethink them of harp and minstrelsy. And all the Muses together with sweet voice in antiphonal chant replying, sing of the imperishable gifts of the Gods, and the sufferings of men, all that they endure from the hands of the undying Gods, lives witless and helpless, men unavailing to find remede for death or buckler against old age. Then the fair-tressed Graces and boon Hours, and Harmonia, and Hebe, and Aphrodite, daughter of Zeus, dance, holding each by the wrist the other's hand, while among them sings one neither unlovely, nor of body contemptible, but divinely tall and fair, Artemis the Archer, nurtured with Apollo. Among them sport Ares, and the keen-eyed Bane of Argos, while Phoebus Apollo steps high and disposedly, playing the lyre, and the light issues round him from twinkling feet and fair-woven raiment. But all they are glad, seeing him so high of heart, Leto of the golden tresses, and Zeus the Counsellor, beholding their dear son as he takes his pastime among the deathless Gods.

How shall I hymn thee aright, howbeit thou art, in sooth, not hard to hymn? Shall I sing of thee in love and dalliance; how thou wentest forth to woo the maiden Azanian, with Ischys, peer of Gods, and Elation's son of the goodly steeds, or with Phorbas, son of Triopes, or Amarynthus, or how with Leucippus and Leucippus' wife, thyself on foot, he in the chariot . . .? {115} Or how first, seeking a place of oracle for men, thou camest down to earth, far-darting Apollo?

On Pieria first didst thou descend from Olympus, and pass by Lacmus, and Emathia, and Enienae, and through Perrhaebia, and speedily camest to Iolcus, and alight on Cenaeum in Euboea, renowned for galleys. On the Lelantian plain thou stoodest, but it pleased thee not there to stablish a temple and a grove. Thence thou didst cross Euripus, far-darting Apollo, and fare up the green hill divine, and thence camest speedily to Mycalessus and Teumesos of the bedded meadow grass, and thence to the place of woodclad Thebe, for as yet no mortals dwelt in Holy Thebe, nor yet were paths nor ways along Thebe's wheat-bearing plain, but all was wild wood.

Thence forward journeying, Apollo, thou camest to Onchestus, the bright grove of Poseidon. There the new-broken colt takes breath again, weary though he be with dragging the goodly chariot; and to earth, skilled though he be, leaps down the charioteer, and fares on foot, while the horses for a while rattle along the empty car, with the reins on their necks, and if the car be broken in the grove of trees, their masters tend them there, and tilt the car and let it lie. Such is the rite from of old, and they pray to the King Poseidon, while the chariot is the God's portion to keep.

Thence faring forward, far-darting Apollo, thou didst win to Cephisus of the fair streams, that from Lilaea pours down his beautiful waters, which crossing, Far-darter, and passing Ocalea of the towers, thou camest thereafter to grassy Haliartus. Then didst thou set foot on Telphusa, and to thee the land seemed exceeding good wherein to stablish a temple and a grove.

Beside Telphusa didst thou stand, and spake to her: "Telphusa, here methinketh to stablish a fair temple, an oracle for men, who, ever seeking for the word of sooth, will bring me hither perfect hecatombs, even they that dwell in the rich isle of Pelops, and all they of the mainland and sea-girt islands. To them all shall I speak the decree unerring, rendering oracles within my rich temple."

So spake Phoebus, and thoroughly marked out the foundations, right long and wide. But at the sight the heart of Telphusa waxed wroth, and she spake her word:

"Phoebus, far-darting Prince, a word shall I set in thy heart. Here thinkest thou to stablish a goodly temple, to be a place of oracle for men, that ever will bring thee hither perfect hecatombs--nay, but this will I tell thee, and do thou lay it up in thine heart. The never-ending din of swift steeds will be a weariness to thee, and the watering of mules from my sacred springs. There men will choose rather to regard the well-wrought chariots, and the stamping of the swift-footed steeds, than thy great temple and much wealth therein. But an if thou--that art greater and better than I, O Prince, and thy strength is most of might--if thou wilt listen to me, in Crisa build thy fane beneath a glade of Parnassus. There neither will goodly chariots ring, nor wilt thou be vexed with stamping of swift steeds about thy well-builded altar, but none the less shall the renowned tribes of men bring their gifts to Iepaeon, and delighted shalt thou gather the sacrifices of them who dwell around."

Therewith she won over the heart of the Far-darter, even that to Telphusa herself should be honour in that land, and not to the Far-darter.

Thenceforward didst thou fare, far-darting Apollo, and camest to the city of the overweening Phlegyae, that reckless of Zeus dwelt there in a goodly glade by the Cephisian mere. Thence fleetly didst thou speed to the ridge of the hills, and camest to Crisa beneath snowy Parnassus, to a knoll that faced westward, but above it hangs a cliff, and a hollow dell runs under, rough with wood, and even there Prince Phoebus Apollo deemed well to build a goodly temple, and spake, saying: "Here methinketh to stablish a right fair temple, to be a place oracular to men, that shall ever bring me hither goodly hecatombs, both they that dwell in rich Peloponnesus, and they of the mainland and sea-girt isles, seeking here the word of sooth; to them all shall I speak the decree unerring, rendering oracles within my wealthy shrine."

So speaking, Phoebus Apollo marked out the foundations, right long and wide, and thereon Trophonius and Agamedes laid the threshold of stone, the sons of Erginus, dear to the deathless Gods. But round all the countless tribes of men built a temple with wrought stones to be famous for ever in song.

Hard by is a fair-flowing stream, and there, with an arrow from his strong bow, did the Prince, the son of Zeus, slay the Dragoness, mighty and huge, a wild Etin, that was wont to wreak many woes on earthly men, on themselves, and their straight-stepping flocks, so dread a bane was she.

[This Dragoness it was that took from golden-throned Hera and reared the dread Typhaon, not to be dealt with, a bane to mortals. Him did Hera bear, upon a time, in wrath with father Zeus, whenas Cronides brought forth from his head renowned Athene. Straightway lady Hera was angered, and spake among the assembled Gods:

"Listen to me, ye Gods, and Goddesses all, how cloud-collecting Zeus is first to begin the dishonouring of me, though he made me his wife in honour. And now, apart from me, he has brought forth grey-eyed Athene who excels among all the blessed Immortals. But he was feeble from the birth, among all the Gods, my son Hephaestos, lame and withered of foot, whom I myself lifted in my hands, and cast into the wide sea. But the daughter of Nereus, Thetis of the silver feet, received him and nurtured him among her sisters. Would that she had done other grace to the blessed Immortals!

"Thou evil one of many wiles, what other wile devisest thou? How hadst thou the heart now alone to bear grey-eyed Athene? Could I not have borne her? But none the less would she have been called thine among the Immortals, who hold the wide heaven. Take heed now, that I devise not for thee some evil to come. Yea, now shall I use arts whereby a child of mine shall be born, excelling among the immortal Gods, without dishonouring thy sacred bed or mine, for verily to thy bed I will not come, but far from thee will nurse my grudge against the Immortal Gods."

So spake she, and withdrew from among the Gods with angered heart. Right so she made her prayer, the ox-eyed lady Hera, striking the earth with her hand flatlings, {121} and spake her word:

"Listen to me now, Earth, and wide Heavens above, and ye Gods called Titans, dwelling beneath earth in great Tartarus, ye from whom spring Gods and men! List to me now, all of you, and give me a child apart from Zeus, yet nothing inferior to him in might, nay, stronger than he, as much as far-seeing Zeus is mightier than Cronus!"

So spake she, and smote the ground with her firm hand. Then Earth, the nurse of life, was stirred, and Hera, beholding it, was glad at heart, for she deemed that her prayer would be accomplished. From that hour for a full year she never came to the bed of wise Zeus, nor to her throne adorned, whereon she was wont to sit, planning deep counsel, but dwelling in her temples, the homes of Prayers, she took joy in her sacrifices, the ox-eyed lady Hera.

Now when her months and days were fulfilled, the year revolving, and the seasons in their course coming round, she bare a birth like neither Gods nor mortals, the dread Typhaon, not to be dealt with, a bane of men. Him now she took, the ox-eyed lady Hera, and carried and gave to the Dragoness, to bitter nurse a bitter fosterling, who received him, that ever wrought many wrongs among the renowned tribes of men.]

Whosoever met the Dragoness, on him would she bring the day of destiny, before the Prince, far-darting Apollo, loosed at her the destroying shaft; then writhing in strong anguish, and mightily panting she lay, rolling about the land. Dread and dire was the din, as she writhed hither and thither through the wood, and gave up the ghost, and Phoebus spoke his malison:

"There do thou rot upon the fruitful earth; no longer shalt thou, at least, live to be the evil bane of mortals that eat the fruit of the fertile soil, and hither shall bring perfect hecatombs. Surely from thee neither shall Typhoeus, nay, nor Chimaera of the evil name, shield death that layeth low, but here shall black earth and bright Hyperion make thee waste away."

So he spake in malison, and darkness veiled her eyes, and there the sacred strength of the sun did waste her quite away. Whence now the place is named Pytho, and men call the Prince "Pythian" for that deed, for even there the might of the swift sun made corrupt the monster. {124}

Then Phoebus Apollo was ware in his heart that the fair-flowing spring, Telphusa, had beguiled him, and in wrath he went to her, and swiftly came, and standing close by her, spoke his word:

"Telphusa, thou wert not destined to beguile my mind, nor keep the winsome lands and pour forth thy fair waters. Nay, here shall my honour also dwell, not thine alone." So he spoke, and overset a rock, with a shower of stones, and hid her streams, the Prince, far-darting Apollo. And he made an altar in a grove of trees, hard by the fair-flowing stream, where all men name him in prayer, "the Prince Telphusian," for that he shamed the streams of sacred Telphusa. Then Phoebus Apollo considered in his heart what men he should bring in to be his ministers, and to serve him in rocky Pytho. While he was pondering on this, he beheld a swift ship on the wine-dark sea, and aboard her many men and good, Cretans from Minoan Cnossus, such as do sacrifice to the God, and speak the doom of Phoebus Apollo of the Golden Sword, what word soever he utters of sooth from the daphne in the dells of Parnassus. For barter and wealth they were sailing in the black ship to sandy Pylos, and the Pylian men. Anon Phoebus Apollo set forth to meet them, leaping into the sea upon the swift ship in the guise of a dolphin, and there he lay, a portent great and terrible.

[Of the crew, whosoever sought in heart to comprehend what he was . . . On all sides he kept swaying to and fro, and shaking the timbers of the galley.] But all they sat silent and in fear aboard the ship, nor loosed the sheets, nor the sail of the black-prowed galley; nay, even as they had first set the sails so they voyaged onward, the strong south-wind speeding on the vessel from behind. First they rounded Malea, and passed the Laconian land and came to Helos, a citadel by the sea, and Taenarus, the land of Helios, that is the joy of mortals, where ever feed the deep- fleeced flocks of Prince Helios, and there hath he his glad demesne. There the crew thought to stay the galley, and land and consider of the marvel, and see whether that strange thing will abide on the deck of the hollow ship or leap again into the swell of the fishes' home. But the well-wrought ship did not obey the rudder, but kept ever on her way beyond rich Peloponnesus, Prince Apollo lightly guiding it by the gale. So accomplishing her course she came to Arene, and pleasant Arguphea, and Thryon, the ford of Alpheius, and well-builded Aepu, and sandy Pylos, and the Pylian men, and ran by Crounoi, and Chalcis, and Dyme, and holy Elis, where the Epeians bear sway. Then rejoicing in the breeze of Zeus, she was making for Pherae, when to them out of the clouds showed forth the steep ridge of Ithaca, and Dulichium, and Same, and wooded Zacynthus. Anon when she had passed beyond all Peloponnesus, there straightway, off Crisa, appeared the wide sound, that bounds rich Peloponnesus. Then came on the west wind, clear and strong, by the counsel of Zeus, blowing hard out of heaven, that the running ship might swiftest accomplish her course over the salt water of the sea.

Backward then they sailed towards the Dawn and the sun, and the Prince was their guide, Apollo, son of Zeus. Then came they to far-seen Crisa, the land of vines, into the haven, while the sea-faring ship beached herself on the shingle. Then from the ship leaped the Prince, far-darting Apollo, like a star at high noon, while the gledes of fire flew from him, and the splendour flashed to the heavens. Into his inmost Holy Place he went through the precious tripods, and in the midst he kindled a flame showering forth his shafts, and the splendour filled all Crisa, {127} and the wives of the Crisaeans, and their fair-girdled daughters raised a wail at the rushing flight of Phoebus, for great fear fell upon all. Thence again to the galley he set forth and flew, fleet as a thought, in shape a man lusty and strong, in his first youth, his locks swathing his wide shoulders. Anon he spake to the seamen winged words:

"Strangers, who are ye, whence sail ye the wet ways? Is it after merchandise, or do ye wander at adventure, over the salt sea, as sea-robbers use, that roam staking their own lives, and bearing bane to men of strange speech? Why sit ye thus adread, not faring forth on the land, nor slackening the gear of your black ship? Sure this is the wont of toilsome mariners, when they come from the deep to the land in their black ship, foredone with labour, and anon a longing for sweet food seizes their hearts."

So spake he, and put courage in their breasts, and the leader of the Cretans answered him, saying:

"Stranger, behold thou art no whit like unto mortal men in shape or growth, but art a peer of the Immortals, wherefore all hail, and grace be thine, and all good things at the hands of the Gods. Tell me then truly that I may know indeed, what people is this, what land, what mortals dwell here? Surely with our thoughts set on another goal we sailed the great sea to Pylos from Crete, whence we boast our lineage; but now it is hither that we have come, maugre our wills, with our galley- -another path and other ways--we longing to return, but some God has led us all unwilling to this place."

Then the far-darting Apollo answered them:

"Strangers, who dwelt aforetime round wooded Cnossus, never again shall ye return each to his pleasant city and his own house, and his wife, but here shall ye hold my rich temple, honoured by multitudes of men. Lo! I am the son of Zeus, and name myself Apollo, and hither have I brought you over the great gulf of the sea, with no evil intent. Nay, here shall ye possess my rich temple, held highest in honour among all men, and ye shall know the counsels of the Immortals, by whose will ye shall ever be held in renown. But now come, and instantly obey my word. First lower the sails, and loose the sheets, and then beach the black ship on the land, taking forth the wares and gear of the trim galley, and build ye an altar on the strand of the sea. Thereon kindle fire, and sprinkle above in sacrifice the white barley-flour, and thereafter pray, standing around the altar. And whereas I first, in the misty sea, sprang aboard the swift ship in the guise of a dolphin, therefore pray to me as Apollo Delphinius, while mine shall ever be the Delphian altar seen from afar. Then take ye supper beside the swift black ship, and pour libations to the blessed Gods who hold Olympus. But when ye have dismissed the desire of sweet food then with me do ye come, singing the Paean, till ye win that place where ye shall possess the rich temple."

So spake he, while they heard and obeyed eagerly. First they lowered the sails, loosing the sheets, and lowering the mast by the forestays, they laid it in the mast-stead, and themselves went forth on the strand of the sea. Then forth from the salt sea to the mainland they dragged the fleet ship high up on the sands, laying long sleepers thereunder, and they builded an altar on the sea-strand, and lit fire thereon, scattering above white barley-flour in sacrifice, and, standing around the altar, they prayed as the God commanded. Anon they took supper beside the fleet black ship, and poured forth libations to the blessed Gods who hold Olympus. But when they had dismissed the desire of meat and drink they set forth on their way, and the Prince Apollo guided them, harp in hand, and sweetly he harped, faring with high and goodly strides. Dancing in his train the Cretans followed to Pytho, and the Paean they were chanting, the paeans of the Cretans in whose breasts the Muse hath put honey-sweet song. All unwearied they strode to the hill, and swiftly were got to Parnassus and a winsome land, where they were to dwell, honoured of many among men.

Apollo guided them, and showed his holy shrine and rich temple, and the spirit was moved in their breasts, and the captain of the Cretans spake, and asked the God, saying:

"Prince, since thou hast led us far from friends and our own country, for so it pleases thee, how now shall we live, we pray thee tell us. This fair land bears not vines, nor is rich in meadows, wherefrom we might live well, and minister to men."

Then, smiling, Apollo, the son of Zeus, spoke to them:

"Foolish ones, enduring hearts, who desire cares, and sore toil, and all straits! A light word will I speak to you, do ye consider it. Let each one of you, knife in right hand, be ever slaughtering sheep that in abundance shall ever be yours, all the flocks that the renowned tribes of men bring hither to me. Yours it is to guard my temple, and receive the tribes of men that gather hither, doing, above all, as my will enjoins. But if any vain word be spoken, or vain deed wrought, or violence after the manner of mortal men, then shall others be your masters, and hold you in thraldom for ever. {133} I have spoken all, do thou keep it in thy heart."

Even so, fare thou well, son of Zeus and Leto, but I shall remember both thee and another song.

II. HERMES

Of Hermes sing, O Muse, the son of Zeus and Maia, Lord of Cyllene, and Arcadia rich in sheep, the fortune-bearing Herald of the Gods, him whom Maia bore, the fair-tressed nymph, that lay in the arms of Zeus; a shamefaced nymph was she, shunning the assembly of the blessed Gods, dwelling within a shadowy cave. Therein was Cronion wont to embrace the fair-tressed nymph in the deep of night, when sweet sleep held white-armed Hera, the immortal Gods knowing it not, nor mortal men.

But when the mind of great Zeus was fulfilled, and over *her* the tenth moon stood in the sky, the babe was born to light, and all was made manifest; yea, then she bore a child of many a wile and cunning counsel, a robber, a driver of the kine, a captain of raiders, a watcher of the night, a thief of the gates, who soon should show forth deeds renowned among the deathless Gods. Born in the dawn, by midday well he harped, and in the evening stole the cattle of Apollo the Far-darter, on that fourth day of the month wherein lady Maia bore him. Who, when he leaped from the immortal knees of his mother, lay not long in the sacred cradle, but sped forth to seek the cattle of Apollo, crossing the threshold of the high-roofed cave. There found he a tortoise, and won endless delight, for lo, it was Hermes that first made of the tortoise a minstrel. The creature met him at the outer door, as she fed on the rich grass in front of the dwelling, waddling along, at sight whereof the luck-bringing son of Zeus laughed, and straightway spoke, saying:

"Lo, a lucky omen for me, not by me to be mocked! Hail, darling and dancer, friend of the feast, welcome art thou! whence gatst thou the gay garment, a speckled shell, thou, a mountain-dwelling tortoise? Nay, I will carry thee within, and a boon shalt thou be to me, not by me to be scorned, nay, thou shalt first serve my turn. Best it is to bide at home, since danger is abroad. Living shalt thou be a spell against ill witchery, and dead, then a right sweet music-maker."

So spake he, and raising in both hands the tortoise, went back within the dwelling, bearing the glad treasure. Then he choked the creature, and with a gouge of grey iron he scooped out the marrow of the hill tortoise. And as a swift thought wings through the breast of one that crowding cares are haunting, or as bright glances fleet from the eyes, so swiftly devised renowned Hermes both deed and word. He cut to measure stalks of reed, and fixed them in through holes bored in the stony shell of the tortoise, and cunningly stretched round it the hide of an ox, and put in the horns of the lyre, and to both he fitted the bridge, and stretched seven harmonious chords of sheep-gut. {136}

Then took he his treasure, when he had fashioned it, and touched the strings in turn with the *plectrum*, and wondrously it sounded under his hand, and fair sang the God to the notes, improvising his chant as he played, like lads exchanging taunts at festivals. Of Zeus Cronides and fair-sandalled Maia he sang how they had lived in loving dalliance, and he told out the tale of his begetting, and sang the handmaids and the goodly halls of the Nymph, and the tripods in the house, and the store of cauldrons. So then he sang, but dreamed of other deeds; then bore he the hollow lyre and laid it in the sacred cradle, then, in longing for flesh of kine he sped from the fragrant hall to a place of outlook, with such a design in his heart as reiving men pursue in the dark of night.

The sun had sunk down beneath earth into ocean, with horses and chariot, when Hermes came running to the shadowy hills of Pieria, where the deathless kine of the blessed Gods had ever their haunt; there fed they on the fair unshorn meadows. From their number did the keen-sighted Argeiphontes, son of Maia, cut off fifty loud-lowing kine, and drove them hither and thither over the sandy land, reversing their tracks, and, mindful of his cunning, confused the hoof-marks, the front behind, the hind in front, and himself fared down again. Straightway he wove sandals on the sea-sand (things undreamed he wrought, works wonderful, unspeakable) mingling myrtle twigs and tamarisk, then binding together a bundle of the fresh young wood, he shrewdly fastened it for light sandals beneath his feet, leaves and all, {138}--brushwood that the renowned slayer of Argos had plucked on his way from Pieria [being, as he was, in haste, down the long way].

Then an old man that was labouring a fruitful vineyard, marked the God faring down to the plain through grassy Onchestus, and to him spoke first the son of renowned Maia:

"Old man that bowest thy shoulders over thy hoeing, verily thou shalt have wine enough when all these vines are bearing. . . . See thou, and see not; hear thou, and hear not; be silent, so long as naught of thine is harmed."

Therewith he drave on together the sturdy heads of cattle. And over many a shadowy hill, and through echoing corries and flowering plains drave renowned Hermes. Then stayed for the more part his darkling ally, the sacred Night, and swiftly came morning when men can work, and sacred Selene, daughter of Pallas, mighty prince, clomb to a new place of outlook, and then the strong son of Zeus drave the broad-browed kine of Phoebus Apollo to the river Alpheius. Unwearied they came to the high- roofed stall and the watering-places in front of the fair meadow. There, when he had foddered the deep-voiced kine, he herded them huddled together into the byre, munching lotus and dewy marsh marigold; next brought he much wood, and set himself to the craft of fire-kindling. Taking a goodly shoot of the daphne, he peeled it with the knife, fitting it to his hand, {140} and the hot vapour of smoke arose. [Lo, it was Hermes first who gave fire, and the fire-sticks.] Then took he many dry faggots, great plenty, and piled them in the trench, and flame began to break, sending far the breath of burning fire. And when the force of renowned Hephaestus kept the fire aflame, then downward dragged he, so mighty his strength, two bellowing kine of twisted horn: close up to the fire he dragged them, and cast them both panting upon their backs to the ground. [Then bending over them he turned them upwards and cut their throats] . . . task upon task, and sliced off the fat meat, pierced it with spits of wood, and broiled it,--flesh, and chine, the joint of honour, and blood in the bowels, all together;--then laid all there in its place. The hides he stretched out on a broken rock, as even now they are used, such as are to be enduring: long, and long after that ancient day. {141a} Anon glad Hermes dragged the fat portions on to a smooth ledge, and cut twelve messes sorted out by lot, to each its due meed he gave. Then a longing for the rite of the sacrifice of flesh came on renowned Hermes: for the sweet savour irked him, immortal as he was, but not even so did his strong heart yield. {141b} . . . The fat and flesh he placed in the high-roofed stall, the rest he swiftly raised aloft, a trophy of his reiving, and, gathering dry faggots, he burned heads and feet entire with the vapour of flame. Anon when the God had duly finished all, he cast his sandals into the deep swirling pool of Alpheius, quenched the embers, and all night long spread smooth the black dust: Selene lighting him with her lovely light. Back to the crests of Cyllene came the God at dawn, nor blessed God, on that long way, nor mortal man encountered him; nay, and no dog barked. Then Hermes, son of Zeus, bearer of boon, bowed his head, and entered the hall through the hole of the bolt, like mist on the breath of autumn. Then, standing erect, he sped to the rich inmost chamber of the cave, lightly treading noiseless on the floor. Quickly to his cradle came glorious Hermes and wrapped the swaddling bands about his shoulders, like a witless babe, playing with the wrapper about his knees. So lay he, guarding his dear lyre at his left hand. But his Goddess mother the God did not deceive; she spake, saying:

"Wherefore, thou cunning one, and whence comest thou in the night, thou clad in shamelessness? Anon, methinks, thou wilt go forth at Apollo's hands with bonds about thy sides that may not be broken, sooner than be a robber in the glens. Go to, wretch, thy Father begat thee for a trouble to deathless Gods and mortal men."

But Hermes answered her with words of guile: "Mother mine, why wouldst thou scare me so, as though I were a redeless child, with little craft in his heart, a trembling babe that dreads his mother's chidings? Nay, but I will essay the wiliest craft to feed thee and me for ever. We twain are not to endure to abide here, of all the deathless Gods alone unapproached with sacrifice and prayer, as thou commandest. Better it is eternally to be conversant with Immortals, richly, nobly, well seen in wealth of grain, than to be homekeepers in a darkling cave. And for honour, I too will have my dues of sacrifice, even as Apollo. Even if my Father give it me not I will endeavour, for I am of avail, to be a captain of reivers. And if the son of renowned Leto make inquest for me, methinks some worse thing will befall him. For to Pytho I will go, to break into his great house, whence I shall sack goodly tripods and cauldrons enough, and gold, and gleaming iron, and much raiment. Thyself, if thou hast a mind, shalt see it."

So held they converse one with another, the son of Zeus of the AEgis, and Lady Maia. Then Morning the Daughter of Dawn was arising from the deep stream of Oceanus, bearing light to mortals, what time Apollo came to Onchestus in his journeying, the gracious grove, a holy place of the loud Girdler of the Earth: there he found an old man grazing his ox, the stay of his vineyard, on the roadside. {144} Him first bespoke the son of renowned Leto.

"Old man, hedger of grassy Onchestus; hither am I come seeking cattle from Pieria, all the crook-horned kine out of my herd: my black bull was wont to graze apart from the rest, and my four bright-eyed hounds followed, four of them, wise as men and all of one mind. These were left, the hounds and the bull, a marvel; but the kine wandered away from their soft meadow and sweet pasture, at the going down of the sun. Tell me, thou old man of ancient days, if thou hast seen any man faring after these cattle?"

Then to him the old man spake and answered:

"My friend, hard it were to tell all that a man may see: for many wayfarers go by, some full of ill intent, and some of good: and it is difficult to be certain regarding each. Nevertheless, the whole day long till sunset I was digging about my vineyard plot, and methought I marked--but I know not surely--a child that went after the horned kine; right young he was, and held a staff, and kept going from side to side, and backwards he drove the kine, their faces fronting him."

So spake the old man, but Apollo heard, and went fleeter on his path. Then marked he a bird long of wing, and anon he knew that the thief had been the son of Zeus Cronion. Swiftly sped the Prince, Apollo, son of Zeus, to goodly Pylos, seeking the shambling kine, while his broad shoulders were swathed in purple cloud. Then the Far-darter marked the tracks, and spake:

"Verily, a great marvel mine eyes behold! These be the tracks of high- horned kine, but all are turned back to the meadow of asphodel. But these are not the footsteps of a man, nay, nor of a woman, nor of grey wolves, nor bears, nor lions, nor, methinks, of a shaggy-maned Centaur, whosoever with fleet feet makes such mighty strides! Dread to see they are that backwards go, more dread they that go forwards."

So speaking, the Prince sped on, Apollo, son of Zeus. To the Cyllenian hill he came, that is clad in forests, to the deep shadow of the hollow rock, where the deathless nymph brought forth the child of Zeus Cronion. A fragrance sweet was spread about the goodly hill, and many tall sheep were grazing the grass. Thence he went fleetly over the stone threshold into the dusky cave, even Apollo, the Far-darter.

Now when the son of Zeus and Maia beheld Apollo thus in wrath for his kine, he sank down within his fragrant swaddling bands, being covered as piled embers of burnt tree-roots are covered by thick ashes, so Hermes coiled himself up, when he saw the Far-darter; and curled himself, feet, head, and hands, into small space [summoning sweet sleep], though of a verity wide awake, and his tortoise-shell he kept beneath his armpit. But the son of Zeus and Leto marked them well, the lovely mountain nymph and her dear son, a little babe, all wrapped in cunning wiles. Gazing round all the chamber of the vasty dwelling, Apollo opened three aumbries with the shining key; full were they of nectar and glad ambrosia, and much gold and silver lay within, and much raiment of the Nymph, purple and glistering, such as are within the dwellings of the mighty Gods. Anon, when he had searched out the chambers of the great hall, the son of Leto spake to renowned Hermes:

"Child, in the cradle lying, tell me straightway of my kine: or speedily between us twain will be unseemly strife. For I will seize thee and cast thee into murky Tartarus, into the darkness of doom where none is of avail. Nor shall thy father or mother redeem thee to the light: nay, under earth shalt thou roam, a reiver among folk fordone."

Then Hermes answered with words of craft: "Apollo, what ungentle word hast thou spoken? And is it thy cattle of the homestead thou comest here to seek? I saw them not, heard not of them, gave ear to no word of them: of them I can tell no tidings, nor win the fee of him who tells. Not like a lifter of cattle, a stalwart man, am I: no task is this of mine: hitherto I have other cares; sleep, and mother's milk, and about my shoulders swaddling bands, and warmed baths. Let none know whence this feud arose! And verily great marvel among the Immortals it would be, that a new-born child should cross the threshold after kine of the homestead; a silly rede of thine. Yesterday was I born, my feet are tender, and rough is the earth below. But if thou wilt I shall swear the great oath by my father's head, that neither I myself am to blame, nor have I seen any other thief of thy kine: be kine what they may, for I know but by hearsay."

So spake he with twinkling eyes, and twisted brows, glancing hither and thither, with long-drawn whistling breath, hearing Apollo's word as a vain thing. Then lightly laughing spake Apollo the Far-darter:

"Oh, thou rogue, thou crafty one; verily methinks that many a time thou wilt break into stablished homes, and by night leave many a man bare, silently pilling through his house, such is thy speech to-day! And many herdsmen of the steadings wilt thou vex in the mountain glens, when in lust for flesh thou comest on the herds and sheep thick of fleece. Nay come, lest thou sleep the last and longest slumber, come forth from thy cradle, thou companion of black night! For surely this honour hereafter thou shalt have among the Immortals, to be called for ever the captain of reivers."

So spake Phoebus Apollo, and lifted the child, but even then strong Argus-bane had his device, and, in the hands of the God, let forth an Omen, an evil belly-tenant, with tidings of worse, and a speedy sneeze thereafter. Apollo heard, and dropped renowned Hermes on the ground, then sat down before him, eager as he was to be gone, chiding Hermes, and thus he spoke:

"Take heart, swaddling one, child of Zeus and Maia. By these thine Omens shall I find anon the sturdy kine, and thou shalt lead the way."

So spake he, but swiftly arose Cyllenian Hermes, and swiftly fared, pulling about his ears his swaddling bands that were his shoulder wrapping. Then spake he:

"Whither bearest thou me, Far-darter, of Gods most vehement? Is it for wrath about thy kine that thou thus provokest me? Would that the race of kine might perish, for thy cattle have I not stolen, nor seen another steal, whatsoever kine may be; I know but by hearsay, I! But let our suit be judged before Zeus Cronion."

Now were lone Hermes and the splendid son of Leto point by point disputing their pleas, Apollo with sure knowledge was righteously seeking to convict renowned Hermes for the sake of his kine, but he with craft and cunning words sought to beguile,--the Cyllenian to beguile the God of the Silver Bow. But when the wily one found one as wily, then speedily he strode forward through the sand in front, while behind came the son of Zeus and Leto. Swiftly they came to the crests of fragrant Olympus, to father Cronion they came, these goodly sons of Zeus, for there were set for them the balances of doom. Quiet was snowy Olympus, but they who know not decay or death were gathering after gold-throned Dawn. Then stood Hermes and Apollo of the Silver Bow before the knees of Zeus, the Thunderer, who inquired of his glorious Son, saying:

"Phoebus, whence drivest thou such mighty spoil, a new-born babe like a Herald? A mighty matter this, to come before the gathering of the Gods!"

Then answered him the Prince, Apollo the Far-darter:

"Father, anon shalt thou hear no empty tale; tauntest thou me, as though I were the only lover of booty? This boy have I found, a finished reiver, in the hills of Cyllene, a long way to wander; so fine a knave as I know not among Gods or men, of all robbers on earth. My kine he stole from the meadows, and went driving them at eventide along the loud sea shores, straight to Pylos. Wondrous were the tracks, a thing to marvel on, work of a glorious god. For the black dust showed the tracks of the kine making backward to the mead of asphodel; but this child intractable fared neither on hands nor feet, through the sandy land, but this other strange craft had he, to tread the paths as if shod on with oaken shoots. {153} While he drove the kine through a land of sand, right plain to discern were all the tracks in the dust, but when he had crossed the great tract of sand, straightway on hard ground his traces and those of the kine were ill to discern. But a mortal man beheld him, driving straight to Pylos the cattle broad of brow. Now when he had stalled the kine in quiet, and confused his tracks on either side the way, he lay dark as night in his cradle, in the dusk of a shadowy cave. The keenest eagle could not have spied him, and much he rubbed his eyes, with crafty purpose, and bluntly spake his word:

"I saw not, I heard not aught, nor learned another's tale; nor tidings could I give, nor win reward of tidings."

Therewith Phoebus Apollo sat him down, but another tale did Hermes tell, among the Immortals, addressing Cronion, the master of all Gods:

"Father Zeus, verily the truth will I tell thee: for true am I, nor know the way of falsehood. To-day at sunrise came Apollo to our house, seeking his shambling kine. No witnesses of the Gods brought he, nor no Gods who had seen the fact. But he bade me declare the thing under duress, threatening oft to cast me into wide Tartarus, for he wears the tender flower of glorious youth, but I was born but yesterday, as well himself doth know, and in naught am I like a stalwart lifter of kine. Believe, for thou givest thyself out to be my father, that may I never be well if I drove home the kine, nay, or crossed the threshold. This I say for sooth! The Sun I greatly revere, and other gods, and Thee I love, and *him* I dread. Nay, thyself knowest that I am not to blame; and thereto I will add a great oath: by these fair-wrought porches of the Gods I am guiltless, and one day yet I shall avenge me on him for this pitiless accusation, mighty as he is; but do thou aid the younger!"

So spake Cyllenian Argus-bane, and winked, with his wrapping on his arm: he did not cast it down. But Zeus laughed aloud at the sight of his evil- witted child, so well and wittily he pled denial about the kine. Then bade he them both be of one mind, and so seek the cattle, with Hermes as guide to lead the way, and show without guile where he had hidden the sturdy kine. The Son of Cronos nodded, and glorious Hermes obeyed, for lightly persuadeth the counsel of Zeus of the AEgis.

Then sped both of them, the fair children of Zeus, to sandy Pylos, at the ford of Alpheius, and to the fields they came, and the stall of lofty roof, where the booty was tended in the season of darkness. There anon Hermes went to the side of the rocky cave, and began driving the sturdy cattle into the light. But the son of Leto, glancing aside, saw the flayed skins on the high rock, and quickly asked renowned Hermes:

"How wert thou of avail, oh crafty one, to flay two kine; new-born and childish as thou art? For time to come I dread thy might: no need for thee to be growing long, thou son of Maia!" {156}

[So spake he, and round his hands twisted strong bands of withes, but they at his feet were soon intertwined, each with other, and lightly were they woven over all the kine of the field, by the counsel of thievish Hermes, but Apollo marvelled at that he saw.]

Then the strong Argus-bane with twinkling glances looked down at the ground, wishful to hide his purpose. But that harsh son of renowned Leto, the Far-darter, did he lightly soothe to his will; taking his lyre in his left hand he tuned it with the *plectrum*: and wondrously it rang beneath his hand. Thereat Phoebus Apollo laughed and was glad, and the winsome note passed through to his very soul as he heard. Then Maia's son took courage, and sweetly harping with his harp he stood at Apollo's left side, playing his prelude, and thereon followed his winsome voice. He sang the renowns of the deathless Gods, and the dark Earth, how all things were at the first, and how each God gat his portion.

To Mnemosyne first of Gods he gave the meed of minstrelsy, to the Mother of the Muses, for the Muse came upon the Son of Maia.

Then all the rest of the Immortals, in order of rank and birth, did he honour, the splendid son of Zeus, telling duly all the tale, as he struck the lyre on his arm. But on Apollo's heart in his breast came the stress of desire, who spake to him winged words:

"Thou crafty slayer of kine, thou comrade of the feast; thy song is worth the price of fifty oxen! Henceforth, methinks, shall we be peacefully made at one. But, come now, tell me this, thou wily Son of Maia, have these marvels been with thee even since thy birth, or is it that some immortal, or some mortal man, has given thee the glorious gift and shown thee song divine? For marvellous is this new song in mine ears, such as, methinks, none hath known, either of men, or of Immortals who have mansions in Olympus, save thyself, thou reiver, thou Son of Zeus and Maia! What art is this, what charm against the stress of cares? What a path of song! for verily here is choice of all three things, joy, and love, and sweet sleep. For truly though I be conversant with the Olympian Muses, to whom dances are a charge, and the bright minstrel hymn, and rich song, and the lovesome sound of flutes, yet never yet hath aught else been so dear to my heart, dear as the skill in the festivals of the Gods. I marvel, Son of Zeus, at this, the music of thy minstrelsy. But now since, despite thy youth, thou hast such glorious skill, to thee and to thy Mother I speak this word of sooth: verily, by this shaft of cornel wood, I shall lead thee re-nowned and fortunate among the Immortals, and give thee glorious gifts, nor in the end deceive thee."

Then Hermes answered him with cunning words:

"Shrewdly thou questionest me, Far-darter, nor do I grudge thee to enter upon mine art. This day shalt thou know it: and to thee would I fain be kind in word and will: but within thyself thou well knowest all things, for first among the Immortals, Son of Zeus, is thy place. Mighty art thou and strong, and Zeus of wise counsels loves thee well with reverence due, and hath given thee honour and goodly gifts. Nay, they tell that thou knowest soothsaying, Far-darter, by the voice of Zeus: for from Zeus are all oracles, wherein I myself now know thee to be all-wise. Thy province it is to know what so thou wilt. Since, then, thy heart bids thee play the lyre, harp thou and sing, and let joys be thy care, taking this gift from me; and to me, friend, gain glory. Sweetly sing with my shrill comrade in thy hands, that knoweth speech good and fair and in order due. Freely do thou bear it hereafter into the glad feast, and the winsome dance, and the glorious revel, a joy by night and day. Whatsoever skilled hand shall inquire of it artfully and wisely, surely its voice shall teach him all things joyous, being easily played by gentle practice, fleeing dull toil. But if an unskilled hand first impetuously inquires of it, vain and discordant shall the false notes sound. But thine it is of nature to know what things thou wilt: so to thee will I give this lyre, thou glorious son of Zeus. But we for our part will let graze thy cattle of the field on the pastures of hill and plain, thou Far- darter. So shall the kine, consorting with the bulls, bring forth calves male and female, great store, and no need there is that thou, wise as thou art, should be vehement in anger."

So spake he, and held forth the lyre that Phoebus Apollo took, and pledged his shining whip in the hands of Hermes, and set him over the herds. Gladly the son of Maia received it; while the glorious son of Leto, Apollo, the Prince, the Far-darter, held the lyre in his left hand, and tuned it orderly with the *plectrum*. Sweetly it sounded to his hand, and fair thereto was the song of the God. Thence anon the twain turned the kine to the rich meadow, but themselves, the glorious children of Zeus, hastened back to snow-clad Olympus, rejoicing in the lyre: ay, and Zeus, the counsellor, was glad of it. [Both did he make one in love, and Hermes loved Leto's son constantly, even as now, since when in knowledge of his love he pledged to the Far-darter the winsome lyre, who held it on his arm and played thereon.] But Hermes withal invented the skill of a new art, the far-heard music of the reed pipes.

Then spake the son of Leto to Hermes thus:

"I fear me, Son of Maia, thou leader, thou crafty one, lest thou steal from me both my lyre and my bent bow. For this meed thou hast from Zeus, to establish the ways of barter among men on the fruitful earth. Wherefore would that thou shouldst endure to swear me the great oath of the Gods, with a nod of the head or by the showering waters of Styx, that thy doings shall ever to my heart be kind and dear."

Then, with a nod of his head, did Maia's son vow that never would he steal the possessions of the Far-darter, nor draw nigh his strong dwelling. And Leto's son made vow and band of love and alliance, that none other among the Gods should be dearer of Gods or men the seed of Zeus. [And I shall make, with thee, a perfect to-ken of a Covenant of all Gods and all men, loyal to my heart and honoured.] {162a} "Thereafter shall I give thee a fair wand of wealth and fortune, a golden wand, three- pointed, which shall guard thee harmless, accomplishing all things good of word and deed that it is mine to learn from the voice of Zeus. {162b} But as touching the art prophetic, oh best of fosterlings of Zeus, concerning which thou inquirest, for thee it is not fit to learn that art, nay, nor for any other Immortal. That lies in the mind of Zeus alone. Myself did make pledge, and promise, and strong oath, that, save me, none other of the eternal Gods should know the secret counsel of Zeus. And thou, my brother of the Golden Wand, bid me not tell thee what awful purposes is planning the far-seeing Zeus.

"One mortal shall I harm, and another shall I bless, with many a turn of fortune among hapless men. Of mine oracle shall he have profit whosoever comes in the wake of wings and voice of birds of omen: he shall have profit of mine oracle: him I will not deceive. But whoso, trusting birds not ominous, approaches mine oracle, to inquire beyond my will, and know more than the eternal Gods, shall come, I say, on a bootless journey, yet his gifts shall I receive. Yet another thing will I tell thee, thou Son of renowned Maia and of Zeus of the AEgis, thou bringer of boon; there be certain Thriae, sisters born, three maidens rejoicing in swift wings. Their heads are sprinkled with white barley flour, and they dwell beneath a glade of Parnassus, apart they dwell, teachers of soothsaying. This art I learned while yet a boy I tended the kine, and my Father heeded not. Thence they flit continually hither and thither, feeding on honeycombs and bringing all things to fulfilment. They, when they are full of the spirit of soothsaying, having eaten of the wan honey, delight to speak forth the truth. But if they be bereft of the sweet food divine, then lie they all confusedly. These I bestow on thee, and do thou, inquiring clearly, delight thine own heart, and if thou instruct any man, he will often hearken to thine oracle, if he have the good fortune. {164} These be thine, O Son of Maia, and the cattle of the field with twisted horn do thou tend, and horses, and toilsome mules. . . . And be lord over the burning eyes of lions, and white-toothed swine, and dogs, and sheep that wide earth nourishes, and over all flocks be glorious Hermes lord. And let him alone be herald appointed to Hades, who, though he be giftless, will give him highest gift of honour."

With such love, in all kindness, did Apollo pledge the Son of Maia, and thereto Cronion added grace. With all mortals and immortals he consorts. Somewhat doth he bless, but ever through the dark night he beguiles the tribes of mortal men.

Hail to thee thus, Son of Zeus and Maia, of thee shall I be mindful and of another lay.

III. APHRODITE

Tell me, Muse, of the deeds of golden Aphrodite, the Cyprian, who rouses sweet desire among the Immortals, and vanquishes the tribes of deathly men, and birds that wanton in the air, and all beasts, even all the clans that earth nurtures, and all in the sea. To all are dear the deeds of the garlanded Cyprian.

Yet three hearts there be that she cannot persuade or beguile: the daughter of Zeus of the AEgis, grey-eyed Athene: not to her are dear the deeds of golden Aphrodite, but war and the work of Ares, battle and broil, and the mastery of noble arts. First was she to teach earthly men the fashioning of war chariots and cars fair-wrought with bronze. And she teaches to tender maidens in the halls all goodly arts, breathing skill into their minds. Nor ever doth laughter-loving Aphrodite conquer in desire Artemis of the Golden Distaff, rejoicing in the sound of the chase, for the bow and arrow are her delight, and slaughter of the wild beasts on the hills: the lyre, the dance, the clear hunting halloo, and shadowy glens, and cities of righteous men.

Nor to the revered maiden Hestia are the feats of Aphrodite a joy, eldest daughter of crooked-counselled Cronos [youngest, too, by the design of Zeus of the AEgis], that lady whom both Poseidon and Apollo sought to win. But she would not, nay stubbornly she refused; and she swore a great oath fulfilled, with her hand on the head of Father Zeus of the AEgis, to be a maiden for ever, that lady Goddess. And to her Father Zeus gave a goodly meed of honour, in lieu of wedlock; and in mid-hall she sat her down choosing the best portion: and in all temples of the Gods is she honoured, and among all mortals is chief of Gods. {168}

Of these she cannot win or beguile the hearts. But of all others there is none, of blessed Gods or mortal men, that hath escaped Aphrodite. Yea, even the heart of Zeus the Thunderer she led astray; of him that is greatest of all, and hath the highest lot of honour. Even his wise wit she hath beguiled at her will, and lightly laid him in the arms of mortal women; Hera not wotting of it, his sister and his wife, the fairest in goodliness of beauty among the deathless Goddesses. To highest honour did they beget her, crooked-counselled Cronos and Mother Rheia; and Zeus of imperishable counsel made her his chaste and duteous wife.

But into Aphrodite herself Zeus sent sweet desire, to lie in the arms of a mortal man. This wrought he so that anon not even she might be unconversant with a mortal bed, and might not some day with sweet laughter make her boast among all the Gods, the smiling Aphrodite, that she had given the Gods to mortal paramours, and they for deathless Gods bare deathly sons, and that she mingled Goddesses in love with mortal men. Therefore Zeus sent into her heart sweet desire of Anchises, who as then was pasturing his kine on the steep hills of many-fountained Ida, a man in semblance like the Immortals. Him thereafter did smiling Aphrodite see and love, and measureless desire took hold on her heart. To Cyprus wended she, within her fragrant shrine: even to Paphos, where is her sacred garth and odorous altar. Thither went she in, and shut the shining doors, and there the Graces laved and anointed her with oil ambrosial, such as is on the bodies of the eternal Gods, sweet fragrant oil that she had by her. Then clad she her body in goodly raiment, and prinked herself with gold, the smiling Aphrodite; then sped to Troy, leaving fragrant Cyprus, and high among the clouds she swiftly accomplished her way.

To many-fountained Ida she came, mother of wild beasts, and made straight for the steading through the mountain, while behind her came fawning the beasts, grey wolves, and lions fiery-eyed, and bears, and swift pards, insatiate pursuers of the roe-deer. Glad was she at the sight of them, and sent desire into their breasts, and they went coupling two by two in the shadowy dells. But she came to the well-builded shielings, {170} and him she found left alone in the shielings with no company, the hero Anchises, graced with beauty from the Gods. All the rest were faring after the kine through the grassy pastures, but he, left lonely at the shielings, walked up and down, harping sweet and shrill. In front of him stood the daughter of Zeus, Aphrodite, in semblance and stature like an unwedded maid, lest he should be adread when he beheld the Goddess. And Anchises marvelled when he beheld her, her height, and beauty, and glistering raiment. For she was clad in vesture more shining than the flame of fire, and with twisted armlets and glistering earrings of flower- fashion. About her delicate neck were lovely jewels, fair and golden: and like the moon's was the light on her fair breasts, and love came upon Anchises, and he spake unto her:

"Hail, Queen, whosoever of the Immortals thou art that comest to this house;

whether Artemis, or Leto, or golden Aphrodite, or high-born Themis, or grey-eyed Athene. Or perchance thou art one of the Graces come hither, who dwell friendly with the Gods, and have a name to be immortal; or of the nymphs that dwell in this fair glade, or in this fair mountain, and in the well-heads of rivers, and in grassy dells. But to thee on some point of outlook, in a place far seen, will I make an altar, and offer to thee goodly victims in every season. But for thy part be kindly, and grant me to be a man pre-eminent among the Trojans, and give goodly seed of children to follow me; but for me, let me live long, and see the sunlight, and come to the limit of old age, being ever in all things fortunate among men."

Then Aphrodite the daughter of Zeus answered him:

"Anchises, most renowned of men on earth, behold no Goddess am I,--why likenest thou me to the Immortals?--Nay, mortal am I, and a mortal mother bare me, and my father is famous Otreus, if thou perchance hast heard of him, who reigns over strong-warded Phrygia. Now I well know both your tongue and our own, for a Trojan nurse reared me in the hall, and nurtured me ever, from the day when she took me at my mother's hands, and while I was but a little child. Thus it is, thou seest, that I well know thy tongue as well as my own. But even now the Argus-slayer of the Golden Wand hath ravished me away from the choir of Artemis, the Goddess of the Golden Distaff, who loves the noise of the chase. Many nymphs, and maids beloved of many wooers, were we there at play, and a great circle of people was about us withal. But thence did he bear me away, the Argus-slayer, he of the Golden Wand, and bore me over much tilled land of mortal men, and many wastes unfilled and uninhabited, where wild beasts roam through the shadowy dells. So fleet we passed that I seemed not to touch the fertile earth with my feet. Now Hermes said that I was bidden to be the bride of Anchises, and mother of thy goodly children. But when he had spoken and shown the thing, lo, instantly he went back among the immortal Gods,--the renowned Slayer of Argus. But I come to thee, strong necessity being laid upon me, and by Zeus I beseech thee and thy good parents,--for none ill folk may get such a son as thee,--by them I implore thee to take me, a maiden as I am and untried in love, and show me to thy father and thy discreet mother, and to thy brothers of one lineage with thee. No unseemly daughter to these, and sister to those will I be, but well worthy; and do thou send a messenger swiftly to the Phrygians of the dappled steeds, to tell my father of my fortunes, and my sorrowing mother; gold enough and woven raiment will they send, and many and goodly gifts shall be thy meed. Do thou all this, and then busk the winsome wedding-feast, that is honourable among both men and immortal Gods."

So speaking, the Goddess brought sweet desire into his heart, and love came upon Anchises, and he spake, and said:

"If indeed thou art mortal and a mortal mother bore thee, and if renowned Otreus is thy father, and if thou art come hither by the will of Hermes, the immortal Guide, and art to be called my wife for ever, then neither mortal man nor immortal God shall hold me from my desire before I lie with thee in love, now and anon; nay, not even if Apollo the Far-darter himself were to send the shafts of sorrow from the silver bow! Nay, thou lady like the Goddesses, willing were I to go down within the house of Hades, if but first I had climbed into thy bed."

So spake he and took her hand; while laughter-loving Aphrodite turned, and crept with fair downcast eyes towards the bed. It was strewn for the Prince, as was of wont, with soft garments: and above it lay skins of bears and deep-voiced lions that he had slain in the lofty hills. When then they twain had gone up into the well-wrought bed, first Anchises took from her body her shining jewels, brooches, and twisted armlets, earrings and chains: and he loosed her girdle, and unclad her of her glistering raiment, that he laid on a silver-studded chair. Then through the Gods' will and design, by the immortal Goddess lay the mortal man, not wotting what he did.

Now in the hour when herdsmen drive back the kine and sturdy sheep to the steading from the flowery pastures, even then the Goddess poured sweet sleep into Anchises, and clad herself in her goodly raiment. Now when she was wholly clad, the lady Goddess, her head touched the beam of the lofty roof: and from her cheeks shone forth immortal beauty,--even the beauty of fair-garlanded Cytherea. Then she aroused him from sleep, and spake, and said:

"Rise, son of Dardanus, why now slumberest thou so deeply? Consider, am I even in aspect such as I was when first thine eyes beheld me?"

So spake she, and straightway he started up out of slumber and was adread, and turned his eyes away when he beheld the neck and the fair eyes of Aphrodite. His goodly face he veiled again in a cloak, and imploring her, he spake winged words:

"Even so soon as mine eyes first beheld thee, Goddess, I knew thee for divine: but not sooth didst thou speak to me. But by Zeus of the AEgis I implore thee, suffer me not to live a strengthless shadow among men, but pity me: for no man lives in strength that has couched with immortal Goddesses."

Then answered him Aphrodite, daughter of Zeus:

"Anchises, most renowned of mortal men, take courage, nor fear overmuch. For no fear is there that thou shalt suffer scathe from me, nor from others of the blessed Gods, for dear to the Gods art thou. And to thee shall a dear son be born, and bear sway among the Trojans, and children's children shall arise after him continually. Lo, AENEAS shall his name be called, since dread sorrow held me when I came into the bed of a mortal man. And of all mortal men these who spring from thy race are always nearest to the immortal Gods in beauty and stature; witness how wise-counselling Zeus carried away golden-haired Ganymedes, for his beauty's sake, that he might abide with the Immortals and be the cup-bearer of the Gods in the house of Zeus, a marvellous thing to behold, a mortal honoured among all the Immortals, as he draws the red nectar from the golden mixing-bowl. But grief incurable possessed the heart of Tros, nor knew he whither the wild wind had blown his dear son away, therefore day by day he lamented him continually till Zeus took pity upon him, and gave him as a ransom of his son high-stepping horses that bear the immortal Gods. These he gave him for a gift, and the Guide, the Slayer of Argus, told all these things by the command of Zeus, even how Ganymedes should be for ever exempt from old age and death, even as are the Gods. Now when his father heard this message of Zeus he rejoiced in his heart and lamented no longer, but was gladly charioted by the wind-fleet horses.

"So too did Dawn of the Golden Throne carry off Tithonus, a man of your lineage, one like unto the Immortals. Then went she to pray to Cronion, who hath dark clouds for his tabernacle, that her lover might be immortal and exempt from death for ever. Thereto Zeus consented and granted her desire, but foolish of heart was the Lady Dawn, nor did she deem it good to ask for eternal youth for her lover, and to keep him unwrinkled by grievous old age. Now so long as winsome youth was his, in joy did he dwell with the Golden-throned Dawn, the daughter of Morning, at the world's end beside the streams of Oceanus, but so soon as grey hairs began to flow from his fair head and goodly chin, the Lady Dawn held aloof from his bed, but kept and cherished him in her halls, giving him food and ambrosia and beautiful raiment. But when hateful old age had utterly overcome him, and he could not move or lift his limbs, to her this seemed the wisest counsel; she laid him in a chamber, and shut the shining doors, and his voice flows on endlessly, and no strength now is his such as once there was in his limbs. Therefore I would not have thee to be immortal and live for ever in such fashion among the deathless Gods, but if, being such as thou art in beauty and form, thou couldst live on, and be called my lord, then this grief would not overshadow my heart.

"But it may not be, for swiftly will pitiless old age come upon thee, old age that standeth close by mortal men; wretched and weary, and detested by the Gods: but among the immortal Gods shall great blame be mine for ever, and all for love of thee. For the Gods were wont to dread my words and wiles wherewith I had subdued all the Immortals to mortal women in love, my purpose overcoming them all; for now, lo you, my mouth will no longer suffice to speak forth this boast among the Immortals, {180} for deep and sore hath been my folly, wretched and not to be named; and distraught have I been who carry a child beneath my girdle, the child of a mortal. Now so soon as he sees the light of the sun the deep-bosomed mountain nymphs will rear him for me; the nymphs who haunt this great and holy mountain, being of the clan neither of mortals nor of immortal Gods. Long is their life, and immortal food do they eat, and they join in the goodly dance with the immortal Gods. With them the Sileni and the keen- sighted Slayer of Argus live in dalliance in the recesses of the darkling caves. At their birth there sprang up pine trees or tall-crested oaks on the fruitful earth, nourishing and fair, and on the lofty mountain they stand, and are called the groves of the immortal Gods, which in no wise doth man cut down with the steel. But when the fate of death approaches, first do the fair trees wither on the ground, and the bark about them moulders, and the twigs fall down, and even as the tree perishes so the soul of the nymph leaves the light of the sun.

"These nymphs will keep my child with them and rear him; and him when first he enters on lovely youth shall these Goddesses bring hither to thee, and show thee. But to thee, that I may tell thee all my mind, will I come in the fifth year bringing my son. At the sight of him thou wilt be glad when thou beholdest him with thine eyes, for he will be divinely fair, and thou wilt lead him straightway to windy Ilios.

But if any mortal man asketh of thee what mother bare this thy dear son, be mindful to answer him as I command: say that he is thy son by one of the flower- faced nymphs who dwell in this forest-clad mountain, but if in thy folly thou speakest out, and boastest to have been the lover of fair-garlanded Cytherea, then Zeus in his wrath will smite thee with the smouldering thunderbolt. Now all is told to thee: do thou be wise, and keep thy counsel, and speak not my name, but revere the wrath of the Gods."

So spake she, and soared up into the windy heaven.

Goddess, Queen of well-stablished Cyprus, having given thee honour due, I shall pass on to another hymn.

IV. HYMN TO DEMETER

Of fair-tressed Demeter, Demeter holy Goddess, I begin to sing: of her and her slim-ankled daughter whom Hades snatched away, the gift of wide- beholding Zeus, but Demeter knew it not, she that bears the Seasons, the giver of goodly crops. For her daughter was playing with the deep-bosomed maidens of Oceanus, and was gathering flowers--roses, and crocuses, and fair violets in the soft meadow, and lilies, and hyacinths, and the narcissus which the earth brought forth as a snare to the fair- faced maiden, by the counsel of Zeus and to pleasure the Lord with many guests. Wondrously bloomed the flower, a marvel for all to see, whether deathless gods or deathly men. From its root grew forth a hundred blossoms, and with its fragrant odour the wide heaven above and the whole earth laughed, and the salt wave of the sea. Then the maiden marvelled, and stretched forth both her hands to seize the fair plaything, but the wide-wayed earth gaped in the Nysian plain, and up rushed the Prince, the host of many guests, the many-named son of Cronos, with his immortal horses. Maugre her will he seized her, and drave her off weeping in his golden chariot, but she shrilled aloud, calling on Father Cronides, the highest of gods and the best.

But no immortal god or deathly man heard the voice of her, . . . save the daughter of Persaeus, Hecate of the shining head-tire, as she was thinking delicate thoughts, who heard the cry from her cave [and Prince Helios, the glorious son of Hyperion], the maiden calling on Father Cronides. But he far off sat apart from the gods in his temple haunted by prayers, receiving goodly victims from mortal men. By the design of Zeus did the brother of Zeus lead the maiden away, the lord of many, the host of many guests, with his deathless horses; right sore against her will, even he of many names the son of Cronos. Now, so long as the Goddess beheld the earth, and the starry heaven, and the tide of the teeming sea, and the rays of the sun, and still hoped to behold her mother dear, and the tribes of the eternal gods; even so long, despite her sorrow, hope warmed her high heart; then rang the mountain peaks, and the depths of the sea to her immortal voice, and her lady mother heard her. Then sharp pain caught at her heart, and with her hands she tore the wimple about her ambrosial hair, and cast a dark veil about her shoulders, and then sped she like a bird over land and sea in her great yearning; but to her there was none that would tell the truth, none, either of Gods, or deathly men, nor even a bird came nigh her, a soothsaying messenger. Thereafter for nine days did Lady Deo roam the earth, with torches burning in her hands, nor ever in her sorrow tasted she of ambrosia and sweet nectar, nor laved her body in the baths. But when at last the tenth morn came to her with the light, Hecate met her, a torch in her hands, and spake a word of tidings, and said:

"Lady Demeter, thou that bringest the Seasons, thou giver of glad gifts, which of the heavenly gods or deathly men hath ravished away Persephone, and brought thee sorrow: for I heard a voice but I saw not who the ravisher might be? All this I say to thee for sooth."

So spake Hecate, and the daughter of fair-tressed Rheie answered her not, but swiftly rushed on with her, bearing torches burning in her hands. So came they to Helios that watches both for gods and men, and stood before his car, and the lady Goddess questioned him:

"Helios, be pitiful on me that am a goddess, if ever by word or deed I gladdened thy heart. My daughter, whom I bore, a sweet plant and fair to see; it was her shrill voice I heard through the air unharvested, even as of one violently entreated, but I saw her not with my eyes. But do thou that lookest down with thy rays from the holy air upon all the land and sea, do thou tell me truly concerning my dear child, if thou didst behold her; who it is that hath gone off and ravished her away from me against her will, who is it of gods or mortal men?"

So spake she, and Hyperionides answered her:

"Daughter of fair-tressed Rheia, Queen Demeter, thou shalt know it; for greatly do I pity and revere thee in thy sorrow for thy slim-ankled child. There is none other guilty of the Immortals but Zeus himself that gathereth the clouds, who gave thy daughter to Hades, his own brother, to be called his lovely wife; and Hades has ravished her away in his chariot, loudly shrilling, beneath the dusky gloom. But, Goddess, do thou cease from thy long lamenting. It behoves not thee thus vainly to cherish anger unassuaged. No unseemly lord for thy daughter among the Immortals is Aidoneus, the lord of many, thine own brother and of one seed with thee, and for his honour he won, since when was made the threefold division, to be lord among those with whom he dwells."

So spake he, and called upon his horses, and at his call they swiftly bore the fleet chariot on like long-winged birds. But grief more dread and bitter fell upon her, and wroth thereafter was she with Cronion that hath dark clouds for his dwelling. She held apart from the gathering of the Gods and from tall Olympus, and disfiguring her form for many days she went among the cities and rich fields of men. Now no man knew her that looked on her, nor no deep-bosomed woman, till she came to the dwelling of Celeus, who then was Prince of fragrant Eleusis. There sat she at the wayside in sorrow of heart, by the Maiden Well whence the townsfolk were wont to draw water. In the shade she sat; above her grew a thick olive-tree; and in fashion she was like an ancient crone who knows no more of child-bearing and the gifts of Aphrodite, the lover of garlands. Such she was as are the nurses of the children of doom-pronouncing kings. Such are the housekeepers in their echoing halls.

Now the daughters of Celeus beheld her as they came to fetch the fair- flowing water, to carry thereof in bronze vessels to their father's home. Four were they, like unto goddesses, all in the bloom of youth, Callidice, and Cleisidice, and winsome Demo, and Callithoe the eldest of them all, nor did they know her, for the Gods are hard to be known by mortals, but they stood near her and spake winged words:

"Who art thou and whence, old woman, of ancient folk, and why wert thou wandering apart from the town, nor dost draw nigh to the houses where are women of thine own age, in the shadowy halls, even such as thou, and younger women, too, who may kindly entreat thee in word and deed?"

So spake they, and the lady Goddess answered:

"Dear children, whoever ye be, of womankind I bid you hail, and I will tell you my story. Seemly it is to answer your questions truly. Deo is my name that my lady mother gave me; but now, look you, from Crete am I come hither over the wide ridges of the sea, by no will of my own, nay, by violence have sea-rovers brought me hither under duress, who thereafter touched with their swift ship at Thoricos where the women and they themselves embarked on land. Then were they busy about supper beside the hawsers of the ship, but my heart heeded not delight of supper; no, stealthily setting forth through the dark land I fled from these overweening masters, that they might not sell me whom they had never bought and gain my price. Thus hither have I come in my wandering, nor know I at all what land is this, nor who they be that dwell therein. But to you may all they that hold mansions in Olympus give husbands and lords, and such children to bear as parents desire; but me do ye maidens pity in your kindness, till I come to the house of woman or of man, that there I may work zealously for them in such tasks as fit a woman of my years. I could carry in mine arms a new-born babe, and nurse it well, and keep the house, and strew my master's bed within the well-builded chambers, and teach the maids their tasks."

So spake the Goddess, and straightway answered her the maid unwed, Callidice, the fairest of the daughters of Celeus:

"Mother, what things soever the Gods do give must men, though sorrowing, endure, for the Gods are far stronger than we; but this will I tell thee clearly and soothly, namely, what men they are who here have most honour, and who lead the people, and by their counsels and just dooms do safeguard the bulwarks of the city. Such are wise Triptolemus, Diocles, Polyxenus, and noble Eumolpus, and Dolichus, and our lordly father. All their wives keep their houses, and not one of them would at first sight contemn thee and thrust thee from their halls, but gladly they will receive thee: for thine aspect is divine. So, if thou wilt, abide here, that we may go to the house of my father, and tell out all this tale to my mother, the deep-bosomed Metaneira, if perchance she will bid thee come to our house and not seek the homes of others. A dear son born in her later years is nurtured in the well-builded hall, a child of many prayers and a welcome. If thou wouldst nurse him till he comes to the measure of youth, then whatsoever woman saw thee should envy thee; such gifts of fosterage would my mother give thee."

So spake she and the Goddess nodded assent. So rejoicing they filled their shining pitchers with water and bore them away. Swiftly they came to the high hall of their father, and quickly they told their mother what they had heard and seen, and speedily she bade them run and call the strange woman, offering goodly hire. Then as deer or calves in the season of Spring leap along the meadow, when they have had their fill of pasture, so lightly they kilted up the folds of their lovely kirtles, and ran along the hollow chariot-way, while their hair danced on their shoulders, in colour like the crocus flower. They found the glorious Goddess at the wayside, even where they had left her, and anon they led her to their father's house. But she paced behind in heaviness of heart, her head veiled, and the dark robe floating about her slender feet divine. Speedily they came to the house of Celeus, the fosterling of Zeus, and they went through the corridor where their lady mother was sitting by the doorpost of the well-wrought hall, with her child in her lap, a young blossom, and the girls ran up to her, but the Goddess stood on the threshold, her head touching the roof-beam, and she filled the doorway with the light divine. Then wonder, and awe, and pale fear seized the mother, and she gave place from her high seat, and bade the Goddess be seated. But Demeter the bearer of the Seasons, the Giver of goodly gifts, would not sit down upon the shining high seat. Nay, in silence she waited, casting down her lovely eyes, till the wise Iambe set for her a well-made stool, and cast over it a glistering fleece. {194} Then sat she down and held the veil before her face; long in sorrow and silence sat she so, and spake to no man nor made any sign, but smileless she sat, nor tasted meat nor drink, wasting with long desire for her deep- bosomed daughter.

So abode she till wise Iambe with jests and many mockeries beguiled the lady, the holy one, to smile and laugh and hold a happier heart, and pleased her moods even thereafter. Then Metaneira filled a cup of sweet wine and offered it to her, but she refused it, saying, that it was not permitted for her to drink red wine; but she bade them mix meal and water with the tender herb of mint, and give it to her to drink. Then Metaneira made a potion and gave it to the Goddess as she bade, and Lady Deo took it and made libation, and to them fair-girdled Metaneira said:

"Hail, lady, for methinks thou art not of mean parentage, but goodly born, for grace and honour shine in thine eyes as in the eyes of doom- dealing kings. But the gifts of the Gods, even in sorrow, we men of necessity endure, for the yoke is laid upon our necks; yet now that thou art come hither, such things as I have shall be thine. Rear me this child that the Gods have given in my later years and beyond my hope; and he is to me a child of many prayers. If thou rear him, and he come to the measure of youth, verily each woman that sees thee will envy thee, such shall be my gifts of fosterage."

Then answered her again Demeter of the fair garland:

"And mayst thou too, lady, fare well, and the Gods give thee all things good. Gladly will I receive thy child that thou biddest me nurse. Never, methinks, by the folly of his nurse shall charm or sorcery harm him; for I know an antidote stronger than the wild wood herb, and a goodly salve I know for the venomed spells."

So spake she, and with her immortal hands she placed the child on her fragrant breast, and the mother was glad at heart. So in the halls she nursed the goodly son of wise Celeus, even Demophoon, whom deep-breasted Metaneira bare, and he grew like a god, upon no mortal food, nor on no mother's milk. For Demeter anointed him with ambrosia as though he had been a son of a God, breathing sweetness over him, and keeping him in her bosom. So wrought she by day, but at night she was wont to hide him in the force of fire like a brand, his dear parents knowing it not. {196} Nay, to them it was great marvel how flourished he and grew like the Gods to look upon. And, verily, she would have made him exempt from eld and death for ever, had not fair-girdled Metaneira, in her witlessness, spied on her in the night from her fragrant chamber. Then wailed she, and smote both her thighs, in terror for her child, and in anguish of heart, and lamenting she spake winged words: "My child Demophoon, the stranger is concealing thee in the heart of the fire; bitter sorrow for me and lamentation."

So spake she, wailing, and the lady Goddess heard her. Then in wrath did the fair-garlanded Demeter snatch out of the fire with her immortal hands and cast upon the ground that woman's dear son, whom beyond all hope she had borne in the halls. Dread was the wrath of Demeter, and anon she spake to fair-girdled Metaneira. "Oh redeless and uncounselled race of men, that know not beforehand the fate of coming good or coming evil. For, lo, thou hast wrought upon thyself a bane incurable, by thine own witlessness; for by the oath of the Gods, the relentless water of Styx, I would have made thy dear child deathless and exempt from age for ever, and would have given him glory imperishable. But now in nowise may he escape the Fates and death, yet glory imperishable will ever be his, since he has lain on my knees and slept within my arms; [but as the years go round, and in his day, the sons of the Eleusinians will ever wage war and dreadful strife one upon the other.] Now I am the honoured Demeter, the greatest good and gain of the Immortals to deathly men. But, come now, let all the people build me a great temple and an altar thereby, below the town, and the steep wall, above Callichorus on the jutting rock. But the rites I myself will prescribe, that in time to come ye may pay them duly and appease my power."

Therewith the Goddess changed her shape and height, and cast off old age, and beauty breathed about her, and the sweet scent was breathed from her fragrant robes, and afar shone the light from the deathless body of the Goddess, the yellow hair flowing about her shoulders, so that the goodly house was filled with the splendour as of levin fire, and forth from the halls went she.

But anon the knees of the woman were loosened, and for long time she was speechless, nay, nor did she even mind of the child, her best beloved, to lift him from the floor. But the sisters of the child heard his pitiful cry, and leapt from their fair-strewn beds; one of them, lifting the child in her hands, laid it in her bosom; and another lit fire, and the third ran with smooth feet to take her mother forth from the fragrant chamber. Then gathered they about the child, and bathed and clad him lovingly, yet his mood was not softened, for meaner nurses now and handmaids held him.

They the long night through were adoring the renowned Goddess, trembling with fear, but at the dawning they told truly to mighty Celeus all that the Goddess had commanded; even Demeter of the goodly garland. Thereon he called into the market-place the many people, and bade them make a rich temple, and an altar to fair-tressed Demeter, upon the jutting rock. Then anon they heard and obeyed his voice, and as he bade they builded. And the child increased in strength by the Goddess's will.

Now when they had done their work, and rested from their labours, each man started for his home, but yellow-haired Demeter, sitting there apart from all the blessed Gods, abode, wasting away with desire for her deep- bosomed daughter. Then the most dread and terrible of years did the Goddess bring for mortals upon the fruitful earth, nor did the earth send up the seed, for Demeter of the goodly garland concealed it. Many crooked ploughs did the oxen drag through the furrows in vain, and much white barley fell fruitless upon the land. Now would the whole race of mortal men have perished utterly from the stress of famine, and the Gods that hold mansions in Olympus would have lost the share and renown of gift and sacrifice, if Zeus had not conceived a counsel within his heart.

First he roused Iris of the golden wings to speed forth and call the fair- tressed Demeter, the lovesome in beauty. So spake Zeus, and Iris obeyed Zeus, the son of Cronos, who hath dark clouds for his tabernacle, and swiftly she sped adown the space between heaven and earth. Then came she to the citadel of fragrant Eleusis, and in the temple she found Demeter clothed in dark raiment, and speaking winged words addressed her: "Demeter, Father Zeus, whose counsels are imperishable, bids thee back unto the tribes of the eternal Gods. Come thou, then, lest the word of Zeus be of no avail." So spake she in her prayer, but the Goddess yielded not. Thereafter the Father sent forth all the blessed Gods, all of the Immortals, and coming one by one they bade Demeter return, and gave her many splendid gifts, and all honours that she might choose among the immortal Gods. But none availed to persuade by turning her mind and her angry heart, so stubbornly she refused their sayings. For she deemed no more for ever to enter fragrant Olympus, and no more to allow the earth to bear her fruit, until her eyes should behold her fair-faced daughter.

But when far-seeing Zeus, the lord of the thunder-peal, had heard the thing, he sent to Erebus the slayer of Argos, the God of the golden wand, to win over Hades with soft words, and persuade him to bring up holy Persephone into the light, and among the Gods, from forth the murky gloom, that so her mother might behold her, and that her anger might relent. And Hermes disobeyed not, but straightway and speedily went forth beneath the hollow places of the earth, leaving the home of Olympus. That King he found within his dwelling, sitting on a couch with his chaste bedfellow, who sorely grieved for desire of her mother, that still was cherishing a fell design against the ill deeds of the Gods. Then the strong slayer of Argos drew near and spoke: "Hades of the dark locks, thou Prince of men out-worn, Father Zeus bade me bring the dread Persephone forth from Erebus among the Gods, that her mother may behold her, and relent from her anger and terrible wrath against the Immortals, for now she contrives a mighty deed, to destroy the feeble tribes of earth-born men by withholding the seed under the earth. Thereby the honours of the Gods are minished, and fierce is her wrath, nor mingles she with the Gods, but sits apart within the fragrant temple in the steep citadel of Eleusis."

So spake he, and smiling were the brows of Aidoneus, Prince of the dead, nor did he disobey the commands of King Zeus, as speedily he bade the wise Persephone: "Go, Persephone, to thy dark-mantled mother, go with a gentle spirit in thy breast, nor be thou beyond all other folk disconsolate. Verily I shall be no unseemly lord of thine among the Immortals, I that am the brother of Father Zeus, and whilst thou art here shalt thou be mistress over all that lives and moves, but among the Immortals shalt thou have the greatest renown. Upon them that wrong thee shall vengeance be unceasing, upon them that solicit not thy power with sacrifice, and pious deeds, and every acceptable gift."

So spake he, and wise Persephone was glad; and joyously and swiftly she arose, but the God himself, stealthily looking around her, gave her sweet pomegranate seed to eat, and this he did that she might not abide for ever beside revered Demeter of the dark mantle. {204} Then openly did Aidoneus, the Prince of all, get ready the steeds beneath the golden chariot, and she climbed up into the golden chariot, and beside her the strong Slayer of Argos took reins and whip in hand, and drove forth from the halls, and gladly sped the horses twain. Speedily they devoured the long way; nor sea, nor rivers, nor grassy glades, nor cliffs, could stay the rush of the deathless horses; nay, far above them they cleft the deep air in their course. Before the fragrant temple he drove them, and checked them where dwelt Demeter of the goodly garland, who, when she beheld them, rushed forth like a Maenad down a dark mountain woodland. {205}

[But Persephone on the other side rejoiced to see her mother dear, and leaped to meet her; but the mother said, "Child, in Hades hast thou eaten any food? for if thou hast not] then with me and thy father the son of Cronos, who has dark clouds for his tabernacle, shalt thou ever dwell honoured among all the Immortals. But if thou hast tasted food, thou must return again, and beneath the hollows of the earth must dwell in Hades a third portion of the year; yet two parts of the year thou shalt abide with me and the other Immortals. When the earth blossoms with all manner of fragrant flowers, then from beneath the murky gloom shalt thou come again, a mighty marvel to Gods and to mortal men. Now tell me by what wile the strong host of many guests deceived thee? . . . "

Then fair Persephone answered her august mother: "Behold, I shall tell thee all the truth without fail. I leaped up for joy when boon Hermes, the swift messenger, came from my father Cronides and the other heavenly Gods, with the message that I was to return out of Erebus, that so thou mightest behold me, and cease thine anger and dread wrath against the Immortals. Thereon Hades himself compelled me to taste of a sweet pomegranate seed against my will. And now I will tell thee how, through the crafty device of Cronides my father, he ravished me, and bore me away beneath the hollows of the earth. All that thou askest I will tell thee. We were all playing in the lovely meadows, Leucippe and Phaino, and Electra, and Ianthe, and Melite, and Iache, and Rhodeia, and Callirhoe, and Melobosis, and Tuche, and flower-faced Ocyroe, and Chraesis, and Ianeira, and Acaste, and Admete, and Rhodope, and Plouto, and winsome Calypso, and Styx, and Urania, and beautiful Galaxaure. We were playing there, and plucking beautiful blossoms with our hands; crocuses mingled, and iris, and hyacinth, and roses, and lilies, a marvel to behold, and narcissus, that the wide earth bare, a wile for my undoing. Gladly was I gathering them when the earth gaped beneath, and therefrom leaped the mighty Prince, the host of many guests, and he bare me against my will despite my grief beneath the earth, in his golden chariot; and shrilly did I cry. This all is true that I tell thee."

So the livelong day in oneness of heart did they cheer each other with love, and their minds ceased from sorrow, and great gladness did either win from other. Then came to them Hekate of the fair wimple, and often did she kiss the holy daughter of Demeter, and from that day was her queenly comrade and handmaiden; but to them for a messenger did far-seeing Zeus of the loud thunder-peal send fair-tressed Rhea to bring dark-mantled Demeter among the Gods, with pledge of what honour she might choose among the Immortals. He vowed that her daughter, for the third part of the revolving year, should dwell beneath the murky gloom, but for the other two parts she should abide with her mother and the other gods.

Thus he spake, and the Goddess disobeyed not the commands of Zeus. Swiftly she sped down from the peaks of Olympus, and came to fertile Rarion; fertile of old, but now no longer fruitful; for fallow and leafless it lay, and hidden was the white barley grain by the device of fair-ankled Demeter. None the less with the growing of the Spring the land was to teem with tall ears of corn, and the rich furrows were to be heavy with corn, and the corn to be bound in sheaves. There first did she land from the unharvested ether, and gladly the Goddesses looked on each other, and rejoiced in heart, and thus first did Rhea of the fair wimple speak to Demeter:

"Hither, child; for he calleth thee, far-seeing Zeus, the lord of the deep thunder, to come among the Gods, and has promised thee such honours as thou wilt, and hath decreed that thy child, for the third of the rolling year, shall dwell beneath the murky gloom, but the other two parts with her mother and the rest of the Immortals. So doth he promise that it shall be and thereto nods his head; but come, my child, obey, and be not too unrelenting against the Son of Cronos, the lord of the dark cloud. And anon do thou increase the grain that bringeth life to men."

So spake she, and Demeter of the fair garland obeyed. Speedily she sent up the grain from the rich glebe, and the wide earth was heavy with leaves and flowers: and she hastened, and showed the thing to the kings, the dealers of doom; to Triptolemus and Diocles the charioteer, and mighty Eumolpus, and Celeus the leader of the people; she showed them the manner of her rites, and taught them her goodly mysteries, holy mysteries which none may violate, or search into, or noise abroad, for the great curse from the Gods restrains the voice. Happy is he among deathly men who hath beheld these things! and he that is uninitiate, and hath no lot in them, hath never equal lot in death beneath the murky gloom.

Now when the Goddess had given instruction in all her rites, they went to Olympus, to the gathering of the other Gods. There the Goddesses dwell beside Zeus the lord of the thunder, holy and revered are they. Right happy is he among mortal men whom they dearly love; speedily do they send as a guest to his lofty hall Plutus, who giveth wealth to mortal men. But come thou that holdest the land of fragrant Eleusis, and sea-girt Paros, and rocky Antron, come, Lady Deo! Queen and giver of goodly gifts, and bringer of the Seasons; come thou and thy daughter, beautiful Persephone, and of your grace grant me goodly substance in requital of my song; but I will mind me of thee, and of other minstrelsy.

V. TO APHRODITE

I shall sing of the revered Aphrodite, the golden-crowned, the beautiful, who hath for her portion the mountain crests of sea-girt Cyprus. Thither the strength of the west wind moistly blowing carried her amid soft foam over the wave of the resounding sea. Her did the golden-snooded Hours gladly welcome, and clad her about in immortal raiment, and on her deathless head set a well-wrought crown, fair and golden, and in her ears put earrings of orichalcum and of precious gold. Her delicate neck and white bosom they adorned with chains of gold, wherewith are bedecked the golden-snooded Hours themselves, when they come to the glad dance of the Gods in the dwelling of the Father. Anon when they had thus adorned her in all goodliness they led her to the Immortals, who gave her greeting when they beheld her, and welcomed her with their hands; and each God prayed that he might lead her home to be his wedded wife, so much they marvelled at the beauty of the fair-garlanded Cytherean. Hail, thou of the glancing eyes, thou sweet winsome Goddess, and grant that I bear off the victory in this contest, and lend thou grace to my song, while I shall both remember thee and another singing.

VI. TO DIONYSUS

Concerning Dionysus the son of renowned Semele shall I sing; how once he appeared upon the shore of the sea unharvested, on a jutting headland, in form like a man in the bloom of youth, with his beautiful dark hair waving around him, and on his strong shoulders a purple robe. Anon came in sight certain men that were pirates; in a well-wrought ship sailing swiftly on the dark seas: Tyrsenians were they, and Ill Fate was their leader, for they beholding him nodded each to other, and swiftly leaped forth, and hastily seized him, and set him aboard their ship rejoicing in heart, for they deemed that he was the son of kings, the fosterlings of Zeus, and they were minded to bind him with grievous bonds. But him the fetters held not, and the withes fell far from his hands and feet. {214} There sat he smiling with his dark eyes, but the steersman saw it, and spake aloud to his companions: "Fools, what God have ye taken and bound? a strong God is he, our trim ship may not contain him. Surely this is Zeus, or Apollo of the Silver Bow, or Poseidon; for he is nowise like mortal man, but like the Gods who have mansions in Olympus. Nay, come let us instantly release him upon the dark mainland, nor lay ye your hands upon him, lest, being wroth, he rouse against us masterful winds and rushing storm."

So spake he, but their captain rebuked him with a hateful word: "Fool, look thou to the wind, and haul up the sail, and grip to all the gear, but this fellow will be for men to meddle with. Methinks he will come to Egypt, or to Cyprus, or to the Hyperboreans, or further far; and at the last he will tell us who his friends are, and concerning his wealth, and his brethren, for the God has delivered him into our hands."

So spake he, and let raise the mast and hoist the mainsail, and the wind filled the sail, and they made taut the ropes all round. But anon strange matters appeared to them: first there flowed through all the swift black ship a sweet and fragrant wine, and the ambrosial fragrance arose, and fear fell upon all the mariners that beheld it. And straightway a vine stretched hither and thither along the sail, hanging with many a cluster, and dark ivy twined round the mast blossoming with flowers, and gracious fruit and garlands grew on all the thole-pins; and they that saw it bade the steersman drive straight to land. Meanwhile within the ship the God changed into the shape of a lion at the bow; and loudly he roared, and in midship he made a shaggy bear: such marvels he showed forth: there stood it raging, and on the deck glared the lion terribly. Then the men fled in terror to the stern, and there stood in fear round the honest pilot. But suddenly sprang forth the lion and seized the captain, and the men all at once leaped overboard into the strong sea, shunning dread doom, and there were changed into dolphins. But the God took pity upon the steersman, and kept him, and gave him all good fortune, and spake, saying, "Be of good courage, Sir, dear art thou to me, and I am Dionysus of the noisy rites whom Cadmeian Semele bare to the love of Zeus." Hail, thou child of beautiful Semele, none that is mindless of thee can fashion sweet minstrelsy.

VII. TO ARES

Ares, thou that excellest in might, thou lord of the chariot of war, God of the golden helm, thou mighty of heart, thou shield-bearer, thou safety of cities, thou that smitest in mail; strong of hand and unwearied valiant spearman, bulwark of Olympus, father of victory, champion of Themis; thou tyrannous to them that oppose thee with force; thou leader of just men, thou master of manlihood, thou that whirlest thy flaming sphere among the courses of the seven stars of the sky, where thy fiery steeds ever bear thee above the third orbit of heaven; do thou listen to me, helper of mortals, Giver of the bright bloom of youth. Shed thou down a mild light from above upon this life of mine, and my martial strength, so that I may be of avail to drive away bitter cowardice from my head, and to curb the deceitful rush of my soul, and to restrain the sharp stress of anger which spurs me on to take part in the dread din of battle. But give me heart, O blessed one, to abide in the painless measures of peace, avoiding the battle-cry of foes and the compelling fates of death.

VIII. TO ARTEMIS

Sing thou of Artemis, Muse, the sister of the Far-darter; the archer Maid, fellow-nursling with Apollo, who waters her steeds in the reedy wells of Meles, then swiftly drives her golden chariot through Smyrna to Claros of the many-clustered vines, where sits Apollo of the Silver Bow awaiting the far-darting archer maid. And hail thou thus, and hail to all Goddesses in my song, but to thee first, and beginning from thee, will I sing, and so shall pass on to another lay.

IX. TO APHRODITE

I shall sing of Cytherea, the Cyprus-born, who gives sweet gifts to mortals, and ever on her face is a winsome smile, and ever in her hand a winsome blossom. Hail to thee, Goddess, Queen of fair-set Salamis, and of all Cyprus, and give to me song desirable, while I shall be mindful of thee and of another song.

X. TO ATHENE

Of Pallas Athene, the saviour of cities, I begin to sing; dread Goddess, who with Ares takes keep of the works of war, and of falling cities, and battles, and the battle din. She it is that saveth the hosts as they go and return from the fight. Hail Goddess, and give to us happiness and good fortune.

XI. TO HERA

I sing of golden-throned Hera, whom Rhea bore, an immortal queen in beauty pre-eminent, the sister and the bride of loud-thundering Zeus, the lady renowned, whom all the Blessed throughout high Olympus honour and revere no less than Zeus whose delight is the thunder.

XII. TO DEMETER

Of fair-tressed Demeter the holy Goddess I begin to sing; of her and the Maiden, the lovely Persephone. Hail Goddess, and save this city and inspire my song.

XIII. TO THE MOTHER OF THE GODS

Sing for me, clear-voiced Muse, daughter of great Zeus, the mother of all Gods and all mortals, who is glad in the sound of rattles and drums, and in the noise of flutes, and in the cry of wolves and fiery-eyed lions, and in the echoing hills, and the woodland haunts; even so hail to thee and to Goddesses all in my song.

XIV. TO HERACLES THE LION-HEART

Of Heracles the son of Zeus will I sing, mightiest of mortals, whom Alcmena bore in Thebes of the fair dancing places, for she had lain in the arms of Cronion, the lord of the dark clouds. Of old the hero wandered endlessly over land and sea, at the bidding of Eurystheus the prince, and himself wrought many deeds of fateful might, and many he endured; but now in the fair haunts of snowy Olympus he dwells in joy, and hath white-ankled Hebe for his wife. Hail prince, son of Zeus, and give to us valour and good fortune.

XV. TO ASCLEPIUS

Of the healer of diseases, Asclepius, I begin to sing, the son of Apollo, whom fair Coronis bore in the Dotian plain, the daughter of King Phlegyas; a great joy to men was her son, and the soother of evil pains. Even so do thou hail, O Prince, I pray to thee in my song.

XVI. TO THE DIOSCOURI

Of Castor and Polydeuces do thou sing,--shrill Muse, the Tyndaridae, sons of Olympian Zeus, whom Lady Leda bore beneath the crests of Taygetus, having been secretly conquered by the desire of Cronion of the dark clouds. Hail, ye sons of Tyndarus, ye cavaliers of swift steeds.

XVII. TO HERMES

I sing of Cyllenian Hermes, slayer of Argus, prince of Cyllene and of Arcadia rich in sheep, the boon messenger of the Immortals. Him did Maia bear, the modest daughter of Atlas, to the love of Zeus. The company of the blessed Gods she shunned, and dwelt in a shadowy cave where Cronion was wont to lie with the fair-tressed nymph in the dark of night, while sweet sleep possessed white-armed Hera, and no Immortals knew it, and no deathly men. Hail to thee, thou son of Zeus and Maia, with thee shall I begin and pass on to another song. Hail, Hermes, Giver of grace, thou Guide, thou Giver of good things.

XVIII. TO PAN

Tell me, Muse, concerning the dear son of Hermes, the goat-footed, the twy-horned, the lover of the din of revel, who haunts the wooded dells with dancing nymphs that tread the crests of the steep cliffs, calling upon Pan the pastoral God of the long wild hair. Lord is he of every snowy crest and mountain peak and rocky path. Hither and thither he goes through the thick copses, sometimes being drawn to the still waters, and sometimes faring through the lofty crags he climbs the highest peak whence the flocks are seen below; ever he ranges over the high white hills, and ever among the knolls he chases and slays the wild beasts, the God, with keen eye, and at evening returns piping from the chase, breathing sweet strains on the reeds. In song that bird cannot excel him which, among the leaves of the blossoming springtide, pours forth her plaint and her honey-sweet song. With him then the mountain nymphs, the shrill singers, go wandering with light feet, and sing at the side of the dark water of the well, while the echo moans along the mountain crest, and the God leaps hither and thither, and goes into the midst, with many a step of the dance. On his back he wears the tawny hide of a lynx, and his heart rejoices with shrill songs in the soft meadow where crocus and fragrant hyacinth bloom all mingled amidst the grass. They sing of the blessed Gods and of high Olympus, and above all do they sing of boon Hermes, how he is the fleet herald of all the Gods, and how he came to many-fountained Arcadia, the mother of sheep, where is his Cyllenian demesne, and there he, God as he was, shepherded the fleecy sheep, the thrall of a mortal man; for soft desire had come upon him to wed the fair- haired daughter of Dryops, and the glad nuptials he accomplished, and to Hermes in the hall she bare a dear son. From his birth he was a marvel to behold, goat-footed, twy-horned, a loud speaker, a sweet laugher. Then the nurse leaped up and fled when she saw his wild face and bearded chin. But him did boon Hermes straightway take in his hands and bear, and gladly did he rejoice at heart. Swiftly to the dwellings of the Gods went he, bearing the babe hidden in the thick skins of mountain hares; there sat he down by Zeus and the other Immortals, and showed his child, and all the Immortals were glad at heart, and chiefly the Bacchic Dionysus. Pan they called the babe to name: because he had made glad the hearts of all of them. Hail then to thee, O Prince, I am thy suppliant in song, and I shall be mindful of thee and of another lay.

XIX. TO HEPHAESTUS

Sing, shrill Muse, of Hephaestus renowned in craft, who with grey-eyed Athene taught goodly works to men on earth, even to men that before were wont to dwell in mountain caves like beasts; but now, being instructed in craft by the renowned craftsman Hephaestus, lightly the whole year through they dwell happily in their own homes. Be gracious, Hephaestus, and grant me valour and fortune.

XX. TO APOLLO

Phoebus, to thee the swan sings shrill to the beating of his wings, as he lights on the bank of the whirling pools of the river Peneus; and to thee with his shrill lyre does the sweet-voiced minstrel sing ever, both first and last. Even so hail thou, Prince, I beseech thee in my song.

XXI. TO POSEIDON

Concerning Poseidon, a great God, I begin to sing: the shaker of the land and of the sea unharvested; God of the deep who holdeth Helicon and wide AEgae. A double meed of honour have the Gods given thee, O Shaker of the Earth, to be tamer of horses and saviour of ships. Hail Prince, thou Girdler of the Earth, thou dark-haired God, and with kindly heart, O blessed one, do thou befriend the mariners.

XXII. TO HIGHEST ZEUS

To Zeus the best of Gods will I sing; the best and the greatest, the far- beholding lord who bringeth all to an end, who holdeth constant counsel with Themis as she reclines on her couch. Be gracious, far-beholding son of Cronos, thou most glorious and greatest.

XXIII. TO HESTIA

Hestia, that guardest the sacred house of the Prince, Apollo the Far-darter, in goodly Pytho, ever doth the oil drop dank from thy locks. Come thou to this house with a gracious heart, come with counselling Zeus, and lend grace to my song.

XXIV. TO THE MUSES AND APOLLO

From the Muse I shall begin and from Apollo and Zeus. For it is from the Muses and far-darting Apollo that minstrels and harpers are upon the earth, but from Zeus come kings. Fortunate is he whomsoever the Muses love, and sweet flows his voice from his lips. Hail, ye children of Zeus, honour ye my lay, and anon I shall be mindful of you and of another hymn.

XXV. TO DIONYSUS

Of ivy-tressed uproarious Dionysus I begin to sing, the splendid son of Zeus and renowned Semele. Him did the fair-tressed nymphs foster, receiving him from the king and father in their bosoms, and needfully they nurtured him in the glens of

Nyse. By his father's will he waxed strong in the fragrant cavern, being numbered among the Immortals. Anon when the Goddesses had bred him up to be the god of many a hymn, then went he wandering in the woodland glades, draped with ivy and laurel, and the nymphs followed with him where he led, and loud rang the wild woodland. Hail to thee, then, Dionysus of the clustered vine, and grant to us to come gladly again to the season of vintaging, yea, and afterwards for many a year to come.

XXVI. TO ARTEMIS

I sing of Artemis of the Golden Distaff, Goddess of the loud chase, a maiden revered, the slayer of stags, the archer, very sister of Apollo of the golden blade. She through the shadowy hills and the windy headlands rejoicing in the chase draws her golden bow, sending forth shafts of sorrow. Then tremble the crests of the lofty mountains, and terribly the dark woodland rings with din of beasts, and the earth shudders, and the teeming sea. Meanwhile she of the stout heart turns about on every side slaying the race of wild beasts. Anon when the Archer Huntress hath taken her delight, and hath gladdened her heart, she slackens her bended bow, and goes to the great hall of her dear Phoebus Apollo, to the rich Delphian land; and arrays the lovely dance of Muses and Graces. There hangs she up her bended bow and her arrows, and all graciously clad about she leads the dances, first in place, while the others utter their immortal voice in hymns to fair-ankled Leto, how she bore such children pre-eminent among the Immortals in counsel and in deed. Hail, ye children of Zeus and fair-tressed Leto, anon will I be mindful of you and of another hymn.

XXVII. TO ATHENE

Of fairest Athene, renowned Goddess, I begin to sing, of the Grey-eyed, the wise; her of the relentless heart, the maiden revered, the succour of cities, the strong Tritogeneia. Her did Zeus the counsellor himself beget from his holy head, all armed for war in shining golden mail, while in awe did the other Gods behold it. Quickly did the Goddess leap from the immortal head, and stood before Zeus, shaking her sharp spear, and high Olympus trembled in dread beneath the strength of the grey-eyed Maiden, while earth rang terribly around, and the sea was boiling with dark waves, and suddenly brake forth the foam. Yea, and the glorious son of Hyperion checked for long his swift steeds, till the maiden took from her immortal shoulders her divine armour, even Pallas Athene: and Zeus the counsellor rejoiced. Hail to thee, thou child of aegis-bearing Zeus, anon shall I be mindful of thee and of another lay.

XXVIII. TO HESTIA

Hestia, thou that in the lofty halls of all immortal Gods, and of all men that go on earth, hast obtained an eternal place and the foremost honour, splendid is thy glory and thy gift, for there is no banquet of mortals without thee, none where, Hestia, they be not wont first and last to make to thee oblation of sweet wine. And do thou, O slayer of Argus, son of Zeus and Maia, messenger of the blessed Gods, God of the golden wand, Giver of all things good, do thou with Hestia dwell in the fair mansions, dear each to other; with kindly heart befriend us in company with dear and honoured Hestia. [For both the twain, well skilled in all fair works of earthly men, consort with wisdom and youth.] Hail daughter of Cronos, thou and Hermes of the golden wand, anon will I be mindful of you and of another lay.

XXIX. TO EARTH, THE MOTHER OF ALL

Concerning Earth, the mother of all, shall I sing, firm Earth, eldest of Gods, that nourishes all things in the world; all things that fare on the sacred land, all things in the sea, all flying things, all are fed out of her store. Through thee, revered Goddess, are men happy in their children and fortunate in their harvest. Thine it is to give or to take life from mortal men. Happy is he whom thou honourest with favouring heart; to him all good things are present innumerable: his fertile field is laden, his meadows are rich in cattle, his house filled with all good things. Such men rule righteously in cities of fair women, great wealth and riches are theirs, their children grow glorious in fresh delights: their maidens joyfully dance and sport through the soft meadow flowers in floral revelry. Such are those that thou honourest, holy Goddess, kindly spirit. Hail, Mother of the Gods, thou wife of starry Ouranos, and freely in return for my ode give me sufficient livelihood. Anon will I be mindful of thee and of another lay.

XXX. TO HELIOS

Begin, O Muse Calliope, to sing of Helios the child of Zeus, the splendid Helios whom dark-eyed Euryphaessa bore to the son of Earth and starry Heaven. For Hyperion wedded Euryphaessa, his own sister, who bore him goodly children, the rosy-armed Dawn, and fair-tressed Selene, and the tireless Helios, like unto the Immortals, who from his chariot shines on mortals and on deathless Gods, and dread is the glance of his eyes from his golden helm, and bright rays shine forth from him splendidly, and round his temples the shining locks flowing down from his head frame round his far-seen face, and a goodly garment wrought delicately shines about his body in the breath of the winds, and stallions speed beneath him when he, charioting his horses and golden-yoked car, drives down through heaven to ocean. Hail, Prince, and of thy grace grant me livelihood enough; beginning from thee I shall sing the race of heroes half divine, whose deeds the Goddesses have revealed to mortals.

XXXI. TO THE MOON

Ye Muses, sing of the fair-faced, wide-winged Moon; ye sweet-voiced daughters of Zeus son of Cronos, accomplished in song! The heavenly gleam from her immortal head circles the earth, and all beauty arises under her glowing light, and the lampless air beams from her golden crown, and the rays dwell lingering when she has bathed her fair body in the ocean stream, and clad her in shining raiment, divine

Selene, yoking her strong-necked glittering steeds. Then forward with speed she drives her deep-maned horses in the evening of the mid-month when her mighty orb is full; then her beams are brightest in the sky as she waxes, a token and a signal to mortal men. With her once was Cronion wedded in love, and she conceived, and brought forth Pandia the maiden, pre-eminent in beauty among the immortal Gods. Hail, Queen, white-armed Goddess, divine Selene, gentle of heart and fair of tress. Beginning from thee shall I sing the renown of heroes half divine whose deeds do minstrels chant from their charmed lips; these ministers of the Muses.

XXXII. TO THE DIOSCOURI

Sing, fair-glancing Muses, of the sons of Zeus, the Tyndaridae, glorious children of fair-ankled Leda, Castor the tamer of steeds and faultless Polydeuces. These, after wedlock with Cronion of the dark clouds, she bore beneath the crests of Taygetus, that mighty hill, to be the saviours of earthly men, and of swift ships when the wintry breezes rush along the pitiless sea. Then men from their ships call in prayer with sacrifice of white lambs when they mount the vessel's deck. But the strong wind and the wave of the sea drive down their ship beneath the water; when suddenly appear the sons of Zeus rushing through the air with tawny wings, and straightway have they stilled the tempests of evil winds, and have lulled the waves in the gulfs of the white salt sea: glad signs are they to mariners, an ending of their labour: and men see it and are glad, and cease from weary toil. Hail ye, Tyndaridae, ye knights of swift steeds, anon will I be mindful of you and of another lay.

XXXIII. TO DIONYSUS

Some say that Semele bare thee to Zeus the lord of thunder in Dracanon, and some in windy Icarus, and some in Naxos, thou seed of Zeus, Eiraphiotes; and others by the deep-swelling river Alpheius, and others, O Prince, say that thou wert born in Thebes. Falsely speak they all: for the Father of Gods and men begat thee far away from men, while white-armed Hera knew it not. There is a hill called Nyse, a lofty hill, flowering into woodland, far away from Phoenicia, near the streams of Ægyptus. . . .

"And to thee will they raise many statues in the temples: as these thy deeds are three, so men will sacrifice to thee hecatombs every three years." {254}

So spake Zeus the counsellor, and nodded with his head. Be gracious, Eiraphiotes, thou wild lover, from thee, beginning and ending with thee, we minstrels sing: in nowise is it possible for him who forgets thee to be mindful of sacred song. Hail to thee, Dionysus Eiraphiotes, with thy mother Semele, whom men call Thyone.

NOTES

{4} Baumeister, p. 94, and note on Hymn to Hermes, 51, citing Antigonus Carystius. See, too, Gemoll, *Die Homerischen Hymnen*, p. 105.

{13} *Journal of Hellenic Society*, vol. xiv. pp. 1-29. Mr. Verrall's whole paper ought to be read, as a summary cannot be adequate.

{16a} Henderson, "The Casket Letters," p. 67.

{16b} Baumeister, "Hymni Homerici," 1860, p. 108 *et seq*.

{18} *Die Homerischen Hymnen*, p. 116 (1886).

{23a} *Journal Anthrop. Inst*., Feb. 1892, p. 290.

{23b} (Op. cit., p. 296.) See "Are Savage Gods Borrowed from Missionaries?" (Nineteenth Century, January 1899).

{24} Hartland, "Folk-Lore," ix. 4, 312; x. I, p. 51.

{30} Winslow, 1622.

{34} For authorities, see Mr Howitt in the *Journal of the Anthropological Institute*, and my "Making of Religion." Also *Folk Lore*, December-March, 1898-99.

{37a} Manning, "Notes on the Aborigines of New Holland." Read before Royal Society of New South Wales, 1882. Notes taken down in 1845. Compare Mrs. Langloh Parker, *More Australian Legendary Tales*, "The Legend of the Flowers."

{37b} Spencer and Gillen, "Natives of Central Australia," p. 651, *s.v.*

{39} For the use of Hermes's tortoise-shell as a musical instrument *without strings*, in early Anahuac, see Prof. Morse, in Appleton's *Popular Science Monthly*, March 1899.

{41} Gemoll.

{44} "Golden Bough," i. 279. Mannhardt, *Antike-Wald-und Feldkulte*, p. 274.

{45} Howitt, *Journal Anthtop. Inst*., xvi. p. 54.

{46a} The Kurnai hold this belief.

{46b} Brough Smyth, vol. i. p. 426

{46c} *Journal Anthrop. Inst*., xvi. pp. 330-331.

{59} The most minute study of Lobeck's *Aglaophamus* can tell us no more than this; the curious may consult a useful short manual, *Eleusis, Ses Mysteres, Ses Ruines, et son Mu-*

see, by M. Demetrios Philios. Athens, 1896. M. Philios is the Director of the Eleusinian Excavations.

{61} "Golden Bough," ii. 292.

{62} "Golden Bough," ii. 369.

{64a} "Golden Bough," ii. 44.

{64b} Ibid., 46.

{65} Mrs. Langloh Parker, "More Australian Legends," pp. 93-99.

{66} The anthropomorphic view of the Genius of the grain as a woman existed in Peru, as I have remarked in "Myth, Ritual, and Religion," i. 213. See, too, "Golden Bough," i. p. 351; Mr. Frazer also notes the Corn Mother of Germany, and the Harvest Maiden of Balquhidder.

{67} "Golden Bough," p. 351, citing from Mannhardt a Spanish tract of 1649.

{68} Howitt, on Mysteries of the Coast Murring (Journal Anthrop. Instit., vol. xiv.).

{69} De Smet, "Oregon Mission," p. 359. Tanner's "Narrative" (1830), pp. 192-193.

{72} Pater, "Greek Studies," p. 90.

{74a} "Africana," i. 130.

{74b} *Journal Anthrop. Instit.* (1884), xiii. pp. 444, 450.

{74c} *Op. cit.*, xiv. pp. 310, 316.

{75} "New South Wales," by Barren Field, pp. 69, 122 (1825).

{76a} Aristophanes, *Ranae*, 445 *et seq.*; Origen. *c. Cels.*, iii. 59; Andocides, *Myst.*, 31; Euripides, *Bacch*, 72 *et seq.* See Wobbermin, *Religionsgeschitliche Studien*, pp. 36-44.

{76b} Wobbermin, *op. cit.*, p. 38.

{77} Wobbermin, *op. cit.*, p. 34.

{78} Hatch, "Hibbert Lectures," pp. 284, 285.

{82} *Recherches sur l'Origine et la Nature des Mysteres d'Eleusis.* Klinikseck. Paris, 1895.

{84} Herodotus, ii. 171.

{85a} Spencer and Gillen, "Natives of Central Australia," p. 399. The myth is not very quotable.

{85b} Foucart, p. 19, quoting *Philosophoumena*, v. 7. M. Foucart, of course, did not know the Arunta parallel.

{85c} *Journal Anthrop. Inst.* (1884), pp. 194, 195, "Ngarego and Wolgal Tribes of New South Wales."

{85d} Ibid. (1885), p. 313.

{86a} For ample information on this head see Mr. Clodd's "Tom-Tit-Tot," and my "Custom and Myth" ("Cupid, Psyche, and the Sun Frog").

{86b} *Panegyr.*, 28.

{87a} Clem. Alex. *Protrept.*, ii. 77 *et seq.*

{87b} Harpocration, *s. v.* [Greek text].

{87c} *Cf.* [Greek text]. Hippon, 90, and Theophrastus, Charact. 6, and Synesius, 213, c. Liddell and Scott, *s.v.* [Greek text].

{88a} "Sand and Spinifex," 1899.

{88b} Foucart, pp. 45, 46

{88c} Hymn, Orph., 41, 5-9.

{89a} Heriot, 1586.

{89b} Foucart, pp. 56-59.

{90} Foucart, p. 64.

{91a} Basil Thomson, "The Kalou-Vu" (Journal Anthrop. Inst., May 1895, pp. 349-356). Mr. Thomson was struck by the Greek analogies, but he did not know, or does not allude to, Plutarch and the Golden Scroll.

{91b} Fragments, V. p. 9, Didot; Foucart, p. 56, note.

{95a} Herodotus, Alilat, i. 131, iii. 8.

{95b} "Cities and Bishoprics of Phrygia," 1895, vol. i. pp. 91, 92.

{104} Callim., H. Apoll. 30.

[Greek verse]

{115} The Greek is corrupt, especially in line 213.

{121} This action was practised by the Zulus in divination, and, curiously, by a Highlander of the last century, appealing to the dead Lovat not to see him wronged.

{124} A folk-etymology from [Greek text] = to rot.

{127} A similar portent is of recent belief in Maori tradition.

{133} See Essay on this Hymn.

{136} In our illustration both the lyre with a tortoise shell for sounding-board, and the cithara, with no such sounding-board, are represented. Is it possible that "the tuneful shell" was primarily used *without* chords, as an instrument for drumming upon? The drum, variously made, is the primitive musical instrument, and it is doubted whether any stringed instrument existed among native American races. But drawings in ancient Aztec MSS. (as Mr. Morse has recently observed) show the musician using a kind of drum made of a tortoise-shell, and some students have (probably with too much fancy) recognised a figure with a tortoise-shell fitted with chords, in Aztec MSS. It is possible enough that the early Greeks used the shell as a sort of drum, before some inventor (Hermes, in the Hymn) added chords and developed a stringed instrument. *Cf.* p. 39.

{138} Such sandals are used to hide their tracks by Avengers of Blood among the tribes of Central Australia.

{140} This piece of wood is that in which the other is twirled to make fire by friction.

{141a} Otherwise written and interpreted, "as even now the skins are there," that is, are exhibited as relics.

{141b} "Der Zweite Halbvers is mir absolut unverstandlich!"--Gemoll.

{144} This is not likely to be the sense, but sense the text gives none. Allen, *Journal of Hellenic Studies*, xvii. II.

{153} "As if one walked with trees instead of feet."--Allen.

{156} The passage which follows (409-414) is too corrupt to admit of any but conjectural rendering. Probably Apollo twisted bands, which fell off Hermes, turned to growing willows, and made a bower over the kine. See Mr. Allen, *op. cit.*

{162a} This passage is a playing field of conjecture; some taking [Greek text] = Mediator, or Go-between: some as = pactum, "covenant."

{162b} There seems to be a reference to the *caduceus* of Hermes, which some have compared to the forked Divining Rod. The whole is corrupt and obscure. To myself it seems that, when he gave the lyre (463-495), Hermes was hinting at his wish to receive in exchange the gift of prophecy. If so, these passages are all disjointed, and 521, with what follows, should come after 495, where Hermes makes the gift of the lyre.

{164} It appears from Philochorus that the prophetic lots were called *thriae*. They are then personified, as the prophetic Sisters, the Thriae. The white flour on their locks may be the grey hair of old age: we know, however, a practice of divining with grain among an early agricultural people, the Hurons.

{168} Hestia, deity of the sacred hearth, is, in a sense, the Cinderella of the Gods, the youngest daughter, tending the holy fire. The legend of her being youngest yet eldest daughter of Cronos may have some reference to this position. "The hearth-place shall belong to the youngest son or daughter," in Kent. See "Costumal of the Thirteenth Century," with much learning on the subject, in Mr. Elton's "Origins of English History," especially p. 190.

{170} Shielings are places of summer abode in pastoral regions.

{180} Reading [Greek text], Mr. Edgar renders "no longer will my mouth ope to tell," &c.

{194} [Greek text] seems to answer to *fauteuil*, [Greek text] to [Greek text].

{196} M. Lefebure suggests to me that this is a trace of Phoenician influence: compare Moloch's sacrifices of children, and "passing through the fire." Such rites, however, are frequent in Japan, Bulgaria, India, Polynesia, and so on. See "The Fire Walk" in my "Modern

Mythology."

{204} An universally diffused belief declares that whosoever tastes the food of the dead may never return to earth.

{205} The lines in brackets merely state the probable meaning of a dilapidated passage.

{214} This appears to answer to the difficult passage about the bonds of Apollo falling from the limbs of Hermes (Hermes, 404, 405). Loosing spells were known to the Vikings, and the miracle occurs among those of Jesuits persecuted under Queen Elizabeth.

{254} There is a gap in the text. Three deeds of Dionysus must have been narrated, then follows the comment of Zeus.

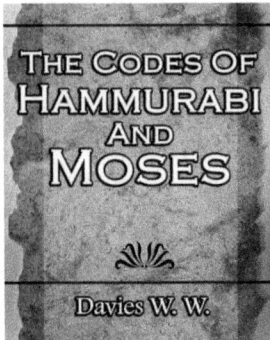

The Codes Of Hammurabi And Moses
W. W. Davies

QTY

The discovery of the Hammurabi Code is one of the greatest achievements of archaeology, and is of paramount interest, not only to the student of the Bible, but also to all those interested in ancient history...

Religion   **ISBN:** *1-59462-338-4*   **Pages:132**
MSRP $12.95

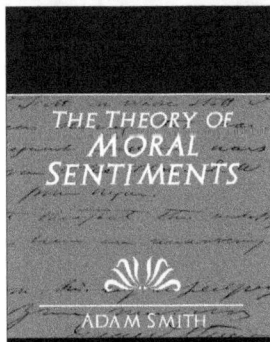

The Theory of Moral Sentiments
Adam Smith

QTY

This work from 1749. contains original theories of conscience amd moral judgment and it is the foundation for systemof morals.

Philosophy **ISBN:** *1-59462-777-0*   **Pages:536**
MSRP $19.95

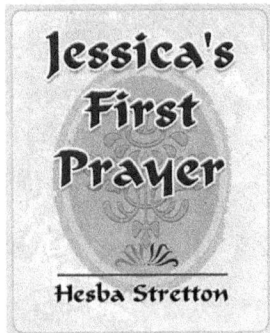

Jessica's First Prayer
Hesba Stretton

QTY

In a screened and secluded corner of one of the many railway-bridges which span the streets of London there could be seen a few years ago, from five o'clock every morning until half past eight, a tidily set-out coffee-stall, consisting of a trestle and board, upon which stood two large tin cans, with a small fire of charcoal burning under each so as to keep the coffee boiling during the early hours of the morning when the work-people were thronging into the city on their way to their daily toil...

Pages:84

Childrens   **ISBN:** *1-59462-373-2*   *MSRP $9.95*

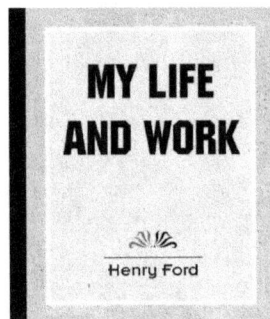

My Life and Work
Henry Ford

QTY

Henry Ford revolutionized the world with his implementation of mass production for the Model T automobile. Gain valuable business insight into his life and work with his own auto-biography... "We have only started on our development of our country we have not as yet, with all our talk of wonderful progress, done more than scratch the surface. The progress has been wonderful enough but..."

Pages:300

Biographies/   **ISBN:** *1-59462-198-5*   *MSRP $21.95*

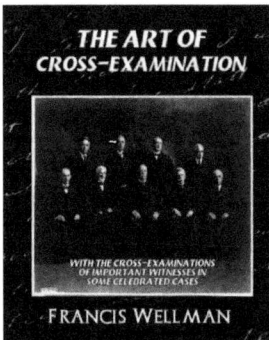

The Art of Cross-Examination
Francis Wellman

QTY

I presume it is the experience of every author, after his first book is published upon an important subject, to be almost overwhelmed with a wealth of ideas and illustrations which could readily have been included in his book, and which to his own mind, at least, seem to make a second edition inevitable. Such certainly was the case with me; and when the first edition had reached its sixth impression in five months, I rejoiced to learn that it seemed to my publishers that the book had met with a sufficiently favorable reception to justify a second and considerably enlarged edition. ..

Pages:412

Reference   ISBN: *1-59462-647-2*   *MSRP $19.95*

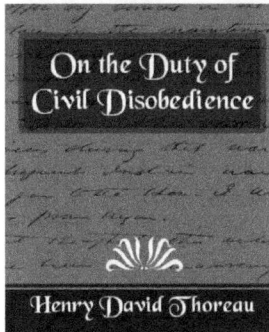

On the Duty of Civil Disobedience
Henry David Thoreau

QTY

Thoreau wrote his famous essay, On the Duty of Civil Disobedience, as a protest against an unjust but popular war and the immoral but popular institution of slave-owning. He did more than write—he declined to pay his taxes, and was hauled off to gaol in consequence. Who can say how much this refusal of his hastened the end of the war and of slavery ?

Law   ISBN: *1-59462-747-9*   **Pages:48**
MSRP $7.45

Dream Psychology Psychoanalysis for Beginners
Sigmund Freud

QTY

Sigmund Freud, born Sigismund Schlomo Freud (May 6, 1856 - September 23, 1939), was a Jewish-Austrian neurologist and psychiatrist who co-founded the psychoanalytic school of psychology. Freud is best known for his theories of the unconscious mind, especially involving the mechanism of repression; his redefinition of sexual desire as mobile and directed towards a wide variety of objects; and his therapeutic techniques, especially his understanding of transference in the therapeutic relationship and the presumed value of dreams as sources of insight into unconscious desires.

Pages:196

Psychology   ISBN: *1-59462-905-6*   *MSRP $15.45*

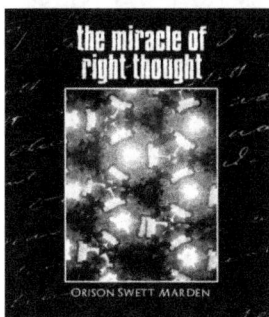

The Miracle of Right Thought
Orison Swett Marden

QTY

Believe with all of your heart that you will do what you were made to do. When the mind has once formed the habit of holding cheerful, happy, prosperous pictures, it will not be easy to form the opposite habit. It does not matter how improbable or how far away this realization may see, or how dark the prospects may be, if we visualize them as best we can, as vividly as possible, hold tenaciously to them and vigorously struggle to attain them, they will gradually become actualized, realized in the life. But a desire, a longing without endeavor, a yearning abandoned or held indifferently will vanish without realization.

Pages:360

Self Help   ISBN: *1-59462-644-8*   *MSRP $25.45*

QTY

The Rosicrucian Cosmo-Conception Mystic Christianity *by Max Heindel*   ISBN: *1-59462-188-8*   **$38.95**
The Rosicrucian Cosmo-conception is not dogmatic, neither does it appeal to any other authority than the reason of the student. It is: not controversial, but is: sent forth in the, hope that it may help to clear...   New Age/Religion Pages 646

Abandonment To Divine Providence *by Jean-Pierre de Caussade*   ISBN: *1-59462-228-0*   **$25.95**
"The Rev. Jean Pierre de Caussade was one of the most remarkable spiritual writers of the Society of Jesus in France in the 18th Century. His death took place at Toulouse in 1751. His works have gone through many editions and have been republished...   Inspirational/Religion Pages 400

Mental Chemistry *by Charles Haanel*   ISBN: *1-59462-192-6*   **$23.95**
Mental Chemistry allows the change of material conditions by combining and appropriately utilizing the power of the mind. Much like applied chemistry creates something new and unique out of careful combinations of chemicals the mastery of mental chemistry...   New Age Pages 354

The Letters of Robert Browning and Elizabeth Barret Barrett 1845-1846 vol II   ISBN: *1-59462-193-4*   **$35.95**
by Robert Browning and Elizabeth Barrett   Biographies Pages 596

Gleanings In Genesis (volume I) *by Arthur W. Pink*   ISBN: *1-59462-130-6*   **$27.45**
Appropriately has Genesis been termed "the seed plot of the Bible" for in it we have, in germ form, almost all of the great doctrines which are afterwards fully developed in the books of Scripture which follow...   Religion/Inspirational Pages 420

The Master Key *by L. W. de Laurence*   ISBN: *1-59462-001-6*   **$30.95**
In no branch of human knowledge has there been a more lively increase of the spirit of research during the past few years than in the study of Psychology, Concentration and Mental Discipline. The requests for authentic lessons in Thought Control, Mental Discipline and...   New Age/Business Pages 422

The Lesser Key Of Solomon Goetia *by L. W. de Laurence*   ISBN: *1-59462-092-X*   **$9.95**
This translation of the first book of the "Lernegton" which is now for the first time made accessible to students of Talismanic Magic was done, after careful collation and edition, from numerous Ancient Manuscripts in Hebrew, Latin, and French...   New Age/Occult Pages 92

Rubaiyat Of Omar Khayyam *by Edward Fitzgerald*   ISDN:*1-59462-332-5*   **$13.95**
Edward Fitzgerald, whom the world has already learned, in spite of his own efforts to remain within the shadow of anonymity, to look upon as one of the rarest poets of the century, was born at Bredfield, in Suffolk, on the 31st of March, 1809. He was the third son of John Purcell...   Music Pages 172

Ancient Law *by Henry Maine*   ISBN: *1-59462-128-4*   **$29.95**
The chief object of the following pages is to indicate some of the earliest ideas of mankind, as they are reflected in Ancient Law, and to point out the relation of those ideas to modern thought.   Religion/History Pages 452

Far-Away Stories *by William J. Locke*   ISBN: *1-59462-129-2*   **$19.45**
"Good wine needs no bush, but a collection of mixed vintages does. And this book is just such a collection. Some of the stories I do not want to remain buried for ever in the museum files of dead magazine-numbers an author's not unpardonable vanity..."   Fiction Pages 272

Life of David Crockett *by David Crockett*   ISBN: *1-59462-250-7*   **$27.45**
"Colonel David Crockett was one of the most remarkable men of the times in which he lived. Born in humble life, but gifted with a strong will, an indomitable courage, and unremitting perseverance...   Biographies/New Age Pages 424

Lip-Reading *by Edward Nitchie*   ISBN: *1-59462-206-X*   **$25.95**
Edward B. Nitchie, founder of the New York School for the Hard of Hearing, now the Nitchie School of Lip-Reading, Inc, wrote "LIP-READING Principles and Practice". The development and perfecting of this meritorious work on lip-reading was an undertaking...   How-to Pages 400

A Handbook of Suggestive Therapeutics, Applied Hypnotism, Psychic Science   ISBN: *1-59462-214-0*   **$24.95**
by Henry Munro   Health/New Age/Health/Self-help Pages 376

A Doll's House: and Two Other Plays *by Henrik Ibsen*   ISBN: *1-59462-112-8*   **$19.95**
Henrik Ibsen created this classic when in revolutionary 1848 Rome. Introducing some striking concepts in playwriting for the realist genre, this play has been studied the world over.   Fiction/Classics/Plays 308

The Light of Asia *by sir Edwin Arnold*   ISBN: *1-59462-204-3*   **$13.95**
In this poetic masterpiece, Edwin Arnold describes the life and teachings of Buddha. The man who was to become known as Buddha to the world was born as Prince Gautama of India but he rejected the worldly riches and abandoned the reigns of power when...   Religion/History/Biographies Pages 170

The Complete Works of Guy de Maupassant *by Guy de Maupassant*   ISBN: *1-59462-157-8*   **$16.95**
"For days and days, nights and nights, I had dreamed of that first kiss which was to consecrate our engagement, and I knew not on what spot I should put my lips..."   Fiction/Classics Pages 240

The Art of Cross-Examination *by Francis L. Wellman*   ISBN: *1-59462-309-0*   **$26.95**
Written by a renowned trial lawyer, Wellman imparts his experience and uses case studies to explain how to use psychology to extract desired information through questioning.   How-to/Science/Reference Pages 408

Answered or Unanswered? *by Louisa Vaughan*   ISBN: *1-59462-248-5*   **$10.95**
Miracles of Faith in China   Religion Pages 112

The Edinburgh Lectures on Mental Science (1909) *by Thomas*   ISBN: *1-59462-008-3*   **$11.95**
This book contains the substance of a course of lectures recently given by the writer in the Queen Street Hall, Edinburgh. Its purpose is to indicate the Natural Principles governing the relation between Mental Action and Material Conditions...   New Age/Psychology Pages 148

Ayesha *by H. Rider Haggard*   ISBN: *1-59462-301-5*   **$24.95**
Verily and indeed it is the unexpected that happens! Probably if there was one person upon the earth from whom the Editor of this, and of a certain previous history, did not expect to hear again...   Classics Pages 380

Ayala's Angel *by Anthony Trollope*   ISBN: *1-59462-352-X*   **$29.95**
The two girls were both pretty, but Lucy who was twenty-one who supposed to be simple and comparatively unattractive, whereas Ayala was credited, as her Bombwhat romantic name might show, with poetic charm and a taste for romance. Ayala when her father died was nineteen...   Fiction Pages 484

The American Commonwealth *by James Bryce*   ISBN: *1-59462-286-8*   **$34.45**
An interpretation of American democratic political theory. It examines political mechanics and society from the perspective of Scotsman James Bryce   Politics Pages 572

Stories of the Pilgrims *by Margaret P. Pumphrey*   ISBN: *1-59462-116-0*   **$17.95**
This book explores pilgrims religious oppression in England as well as their escape to Holland and eventual crossing to America on the Mayflower, and their early days in New England...   History Pages 268

QTY

The Fasting Cure by *Sinclair Upton*   ISBN: *1-59462-222-1*   **$13.95**
In the Cosmopolitan Magazine for May, 1910, and in the Contemporary Review (London) for April, 1910, I published an article dealing with my experiences in fasting. I have written a great many magazine articles, but never one which attracted so much attention...   New Age/Self Help/Health Pages 164

Hebrew Astrology by *Sepharial*   ISBN: *1-59462-308-2*   **$13.45**
In these days of advanced thinking it is a matter of common observation that we have left many of the old landmarks behind and that we are now pressing forward to greater heights and to a wider horizon than that which represented the mind-content of our progenitors...   Astrology Pages 144

Thought Vibration or The Law of Attraction in the Thought World   ISBN: *1-59462-127-6*   **$12.95**
by *William Walker Atkinson*   *Psychology/Religion Pages 144*

Optimism by *Helen Keller*   ISBN: *1-59462-108-X*   **$15.95**
Helen Keller was blind, deaf, and mute since 19 months old, yet famously learned how to overcome these handicaps, communicate with the world, and spread her lectures promoting optimism. An inspiring read for everyone...   Biographies/Inspirational Pages 84

Sara Crewe by *Frances Burnett*   ISBN: *1-59462-360-0*   **$9.45**
In the first place, Miss Minchin lived in London. Her home was a large, dull, tall one, in a large, dull square, where all the houses were alike, and all the sparrows were alike, and where all the door-knockers made the same heavy sound...   Childrens/Classic Pages 88

The Autobiography of Benjamin Franklin by *Benjamin Franklin*   ISBN: *1-59462-135-7*   **$24.95**
The Autobiography of Benjamin Franklin has probably been more extensively read than any other American historical work, and no other book of its kind has had such ups and downs of fortune. Franklin lived for many years in England, where he was agent...   Biographies/History Pages 332

Name	
Email	
Telephone	
Address	
City, State ZIP	

☐ **Credit Card**   ☐ **Check / Money Order**

Credit Card Number	
Expiration Date	
Signature	

Please Mail to: Book Jungle
PO Box 2226
Champaign, IL 61825
or Fax to: 630-214-0564

ORDERING INFORMATION
web*: www.bookjungle.com*
email*: sales@bookjungle.com*
fax*: 630-214-0564*
mail*: Book Jungle PO Box 2226 Champaign, IL 61825*
or PayPal *to sales@bookjungle.com*

Please contact us for bulk discounts

DIRECT-ORDER TERMS
20% Discount if You Order Two or More Books
Free Domestic Shipping!
Accepted: Master Card, Visa, Discover, American Express

www.ingramcontent.com/pod-product-compliance
Lightning Source LLC
LaVergne TN
LVHW081324060426
835511LV00011B/1842